STRENGTHS
IN MAKING DISCIPLES

Thoughts and Tips
For Change Agents

Baha Habashy

and

Margaret Habashy

Published by Integrity+ Consulting

24 Dewitt Court, Markham, Ontario, Canada L3P 3Y3

Phone: (905) 294-0380

E-mail: info@integrity-plus.com

Library and Archives Canada Cataloguing in Publication

Habashy, Baha, 1942-

STRENGTHS IN MAKING DISCIPLES: Thoughts, Tips, and Tools for Change Agents/ Baha Habashy with Margaret Habashy

ISBN 978-0-9939302-6-3

Cataloging Data:

Leadership, Discipleships, Christian Living, Church, StrengthsFinder2.0,

Also available in PDF

This Book Is Dedicated

To the disciple-makers
who invested in teaching us,

To the small group facilitators
where we learned to study God's word, and

To the coaches who gave of themselves
through the good and hard times of life,

And to our spiritual parents,

Carl and Gloria Crate

and

Grace and Ernest LaFont.

Thank you for leading us into
a personal relationship with Jesus.

ABOUT THIS BOOK

When Christ calls us to go and make disciples, He is calling us into a relationship with Himself and with those we meet on the road of life. This book is an imperfect tool that could help those seeking to be intentional in building relationships and making disciples.

Thoughts and Tips for Change Agents

This book is from two imperfect people who seek to follow the command of Paul when he instructed Timothy saying, *"And the things that thou hast heard of me among many witnesses, the same commit thou to faithful men, who shall be able to teach others also."* 2 Timothy 2:2. Through the following pages we seek to provide:

- Lessons God has tried and continues to teach us. We confess that we often fail to apply some of the thoughts and tips we have recorded here. But God is faithful and continues to forgive us.

- Stories of people we met on the road of life. These are provided to illustrate the application of the thoughts, tips, and tools we are pleased to offer you. These stories we adapted from true life experiences while changing the names for confidentiality.

- A self-study toolset. As you go through it, PLEASE do not do it alone. Do it with Jesus at your side. He can compensate for our imperfections. Prayerfully ask Him to guide you as you personalize its thoughts, apply its tips, and use the tools we have provided.

CONTENTS

TOOLS and RESOURCES

INTRODUCTION

Adam came to church on Sunday full of anticipation. It was the last Sunday of the annual church mission's month. The Lord motivated him to give the funds he received from the sale of one of his small businesses to the service of the Kingdom of God.

The service started well. The worshipful songs were full of praise to the Lord's power and grace. The scripture reading was Matthew 28:18-20, *"Then Jesus came to them and said, "All authority in heaven and on earth has been given to me. Therefore, go and make disciples of all nations, baptizing them in the name of the Father and of the Son and the Holy Spirit, and teaching them to obey everything I have commanded you. And surely, I am with you always, to the very end of the age."*

For the sermon, the pastor had invited a guest preacher who was passionate, animated, and very loud. For emphasis, the preacher read the Matthew 28 passage again. The loud preacher spoke for more than 40 minutes, leaving Adam confused and frustrated. There were a few words the preacher repeated several times. ***"If you are not making disciples, you are not a disciple."***

Adam left church feeling deflated and downhearted. Driving home, he thought to himself, *"Based on what that preacher said, am I a disciple? Where or when have I ever been making disciples?"*

Adam's journey started in a home where his Dad was rather hostile to Christians. As a result, he had no contact with the church or Christians until his second year in university when he was invited to a group on campus. Initially, he started going out of curiosity but later because of his interest in one specific young lady.

He was very surprised when she told him that she liked him very much but would not go out with him because he was not a Christian. This challenged him to examine the claims of Christ for himself. His journey of discovery led him to faith in Christ and he started attending church regularly.

It was at church that he met Jane and fell in love with her. 18 months later they were married. Church had become a part of their family life and traditions. While he was not as involved as his wife, he was in church every Sunday unless he was out of town on business. He has been very successful as a businessman. He had been generous in giving to the church and global missions.

In the church, he struggled with a bit of self-esteem, especially when compared to his wife. She was the one involved in a lot of activities. Talking to himself he said, "*I never preached a sermon or baptized anyone. I was never asked to teach Sunday school, lead a Bible study, or serve on any church committee. I never shared the gospel with anyone and never had the great joy of leading someone to the Lord. No one ever asked me to make disciples. Can I call myself a disciple if I am not making disciples? Can I honestly say that I am a Christian?*"

Later that evening Adam shared his concerns with his wife. Trying to support him she reminded him that he plays important roles serving on the board of 4 different charities. While he appreciated her support, her comment left him unconvinced.

What Did Jesus Mean?

What did Jesus mean when He said, "... ***go and make disciples of all nations?***" I suspect the same perplexing question must have gone through the minds of the disciples that day after Jesus left them. Here was a group of ordinary men who left everything and lived the past 3 years in the shadow of their great master. Now He left them and He

> *Making disciples is being intentionally engaged in the process of making His kingdom come on earth as it is in heaven.*

wanted them to **teach all He had said.** How can they even remember all He had taught them in 3 full years? They have lived in a tiny part of the vast Roman empire and have never sailed the high seas and now He wanted them to go to make disciples of **all nations**.

What did Jesus mean when he said, "*... go and make disciples of all nations?*" Do these instructions apply to each of us or a selected few? Is there truth to what that preacher said, *"If you are not making disciples, you are not a disciple."*

Through the pages of this simple booklet, we will seek to examine these questions. As we do this we will consider the roles Jesus played and the model He has set before us. It is our hope is that you will see that making disciples is being intentionally engaged in the process of making His kingdom come on earth as it is in heaven.

Question:

- Do you agree or disagree with what the preacher said? *"If you are not making disciples, you are not a disciple."* Why?
- What would you tell Adam if he came seeking your advice?
- Have you started the journey of being a true disciple of Jesus?

The most important question you need to answer before you consider anything about making disciples is, "Have you started the journey of being a true disciple of Jesus?"

If you are not sure, please watch the short video at

https://youtu.be/6Y_MQMR8dWI

FOUNDATIONS

What Is Making Disciples?

Why did Jesus leave His eternal glory and come to our sinful world?

Through the Lord's prayer, He made His purpose very clear and He wants us to seek after the same Purpose by teaching us to pray. *"May Your Kingdom come, Your will be done on earth as it is in heaven."* Matthew 6:9. What is the kingdom of God and what is the will of God?

Pastor Steve Shaw has quoted, *"The Kingdom of God and the will of God are the same thing. God's will is to restore God's world through God's people in God's time."* God's will is to restore the whole world beginning with yours and mine. In this, we become His disciples.

Restoration always requires major change. How does it happen? According to the author, Dallas Willard, *"Discipleship is being with Jesus to learn from Jesus how to become like Jesus."* Jesus is our model change agent. If this is true, then making disciples is doing what Jesus did to change the world. By telling us "… go and make disciples" He is calling us to be change agents like Him.

JESUS, THE MODEL CHANGE AGENT

*He was born in an obscure
  village
The child of a peasant
  woman
He grew up in another
  obscure village
Where he worked in a
  carpenter shop
Until he was thirty
He never wrote a book
He never held an office
He never went to college
He never visited a big city
He never traveled more
  than two hundred miles
From the place where he
  was born
He did none of the things
Usually associated with
  greatness
He had no credentials but
  himself
He was only thirty-three
His friends ran away
One of them denied him
He was turned over to his
  enemies
And went through the
  mockery of a trial
He was nailed to a cross
  between two thieves*

*While dying, his
  executioners gambled for
  his clothing
The only property he had
  on earth
When he was dead
He was laid in a borrowed
  grave
Through the pity of a friend
Nineteen centuries have
  come and gone
And today Jesus is the
  central figure of the
  human race
And the leader of mankind's
  progress
All the armies that have
  ever marched
All the navies that have
  ever sailed
All the parliaments that
  have ever sat
All the kings that ever
  reigned put together
Have not affected the life
  of mankind on earth
As powerfully as that one
  solitary life.*

Dr. James Allan © 1926

WHAT DID JESUS DO?

If Jesus was such an amazing change agent, why didn't he change the world through His time on earth? After all, did he not say that *"All authority was given to him."* If he did not change everyone He encountered, why does He expect you and me to change the world?

Although Jesus had all authority and power, and still does, He only changes the lives of those who are willing to be changed. For example, in Matthew 19:22 we read that *"a man came up to Jesus and asked, "Teacher, what good thing must I do to get eternal life?... Jesus replied, 'If you want to be perfect, go, sell your possessions and give to the poor, and you will have treasure in heaven. Then come, follow me.' When the young man heard this, he went away sad, because he had great wealth."* On the other hand, we read about Zacchaeus, the fraudulent tax collector, who after meeting Jesus said, *"Lord, half of my goods I give to the poor; and if I have taken anything from any man by false accusation, I restore him fourfold."* Luke 19:8. We also read about Peter, James, and John, who left everything and followed Him. Jesus changed the lives of those who were willing to be changed.

If He has changed your life, you will know that He did not force you to change. Rather He changed you because you were willing and able to change. Jesus understood that change is a process. In making disciples you and I need to be aware of the process of change. Later we will discuss how the strengths resources can help you lead people through this process of change.

What Is the Change Process?

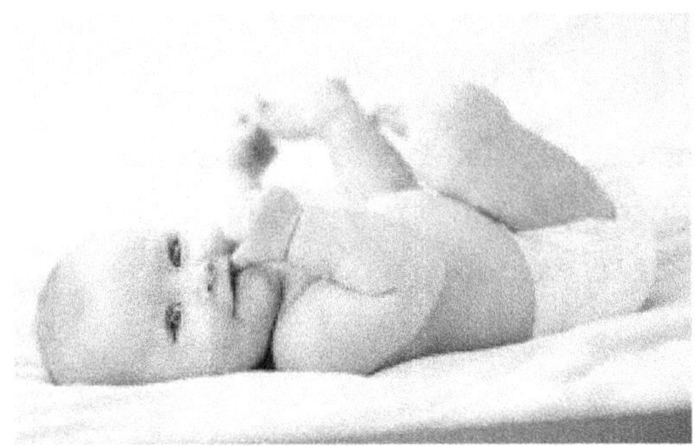

Please give me your vote. Do you agree or disagree with the following statement? ***"The only person who likes change is a baby with a wet diaper."***

If you voted **"agree"**, you could be correct because most of us have a natural propensity to keeping the status quo.

If you voted **"disagree"**, you are most likely correct because most of us would like a change that will include improved wellbeing, better health, quality family life, richer bank account, a newer car … What makes a difference? We all like good change but most of us do not like the process of change or the price of change.

Life is all about change. We must change as we grow. We need to change as the world changes around us. How we respond to our changing world is critical to our wellbeing. If we do not respond to our changing world, we face negative and even dangerous consequences.

Like a good parent, God desires healthy change for His children. God delights in seeing His children grow as they respond to their changing world and His calling on their lives.

When we face life challenges or want to take advantage of great opportunities, most of us need support, encouragement, and/or accountability. To help us achieve the desired change, we need people who partner with us. In previous generations, this was the role of healthy extended family members. Today this role is often relegated to friends, pastors, facilitators, and coaches. At some stage in our lives, most of us will have people who need our support or help in negotiating life changes. This is your chance to partner with Jesus in helping someone change. This is your chance to play a role in the process of making disciples.

Healthy change comes from an **idea** that changes to a **desire** to change, then to a **willingness** to change, and finally to the **ability** to change. This leads to creating and executing a plan to change.

- **The idea to change:** Nothing happens without a good thought or a good idea. Sometimes we call this having a vision of the desired state based on a need or opportunity.

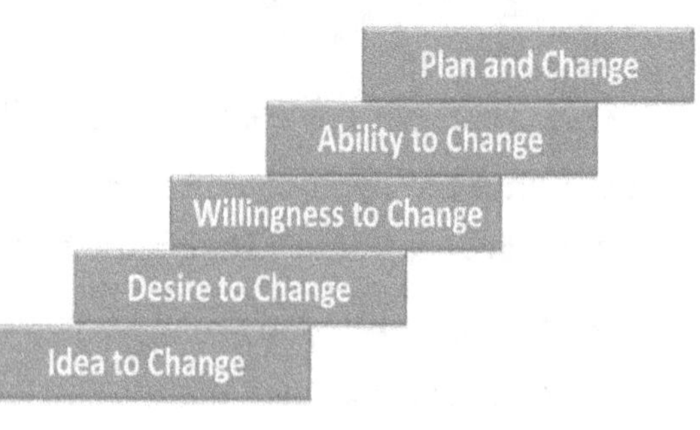

- **Desire to change:** The desire to change happens when our emotions are engaged in the process to support our thinking or rational mind. As we envision the benefits of change or the negative consequences of continuing our life without change, we are energized and motivated to move into the next step.

- **Willingness to change:** Change has a price. All change good or bad has a price. Willingness to change happens when we are willing to pay the price of change. The price for change is directly related to the expected benefits or the cost avoidance associated with the change.

> *Making disciples is being intentionally engaged in helping people in the process of making change.*

- **Ability to change:** Ability goes beyond a willingness to pay the price to change. This is often related to cultural factors or elements beyond personal controls. Most often this leads to adjusting the idea or the scope of the needed change, or even making peace with reality and accepting the status quo.

- **Plan to change:** Having climbed the first four steps, a person is ready to make an educated, reasonable plan to change. In the absence of the first four steps, most plans are temporary or imperfect at best.

Do You Know Sam?

To illustrate the difference between idea, desire, willingness, and ability to change, let me tell you about Sam. Sam sent me an e-mail asking if I could meet with him. This happened at the recommendation of his pastor who told him that I help people with the problem of e-mail and information overload.

Sam was the CEO of a fast-growing company. He first contacted me because he had an idea. During our initial conversation, Sam told me he spent too much time on e-mail and found it a waste of time. His office was cluttered with books, papers, and all sorts of things on his desk. Our conversation uncovered the real cause of his overloaded life. Under his leadership, the business has experienced a 400% growth. Now he works more than 75 hours a week and seldom takes a day off. Although the company has added extra staff his role has not changed much.

During our conversation, Sam could see that his problem was **"Overloaded roles"** much more than e-mail or information overload. As we talked Sam began to see that he had become a workaholic, but he was not convinced of the need to make major changes to his work life. Ending our meeting, I offered to meet with him again only if he would give serious consideration to the following two questions:

1. What will your life be like in 10 years if you continue in this overloaded state of life?
2. If solving your overload problem saved you 10 hours a week, what would you do with that extra time?

During the following weeks, I prayed for Sam. I asked God to do the work that I could not do in his life. I was not surprised when a few weeks later Sam called saying that he had been praying and thinking about the two questions and invited me to have lunch with him.

During our lunch, Sam told me that on the second question he does not have an answer. Other than working, he had a hard time envisioning what he would do with any spare time. For more than 20 years, his life was focused on his work. He loved his work and could not see himself doing anything else. He does not even enjoy taking holidays.

I asked him about the first question. He said, ***"Thinking of what would happen if I do not change frightened me."*** He told me his medical profile puts him at a very high risk of a heart attack. His doctor and his wife have warned him repeatedly. His younger brother died leaving behind three young fatherless children. As he pondered this, Sam began to move from **idea** to change to **desire** to change. Our lunch continued as we discussed the **willingness** to change and the price he will have to pay.

As we talked about the changes, he needed to make he said, "Change will be hard but I am **willing to do it**." He asked me to help him. We created a three-month coaching project to reduce his work life to no more than 60 hours a week. This would require a change in his roles and responsibilities. On the surface Sam was willing to make the changes we agreed on.

Regretfully, he was unable to change. Why? The corporate culture has turned him into a micromanager and his management team and his board were used to this and would not support him in making the needed changes. His workaholic lifestyle was fuelling his adrenalin addiction which hindered his **ability to change.**

Six years later I learned that Sam had major heart surgery. I called him to see how he was doing. He was still at home recovering. He thanked me for my call and told me that when he is ready to go back to work, he will be giving up his CEO role. He would like to accept a less demanding job and work only 3 days a week. I agreed that, when he is ready, I will be there to support him in making that transition.   At that time, I knew Sam would follow through with the plan to change.

Why Do People Change?

When we examine the 3 years that Jesus spent in ministry, we will note that most of the people that He impacted came to Him because they had well defined or obvious needs or desires.   The same applies to you and me as we seek to help people change.   We can spend a lot of time trying to identify reasons that could drive people to change.   On the other hand, key indicators of common symptoms or issues that face the majority of people you and I meet every day already exist.   There are two areas of needs that affect the majority of people in our developing world.   These are low lying fruits that we wish to focus on as we consider Strengths as a tool in making disciples.

> *Making disciples is being intentionally engaged in meeting needs.*

The Need for Self Esteem

In Genesis 1:26 God said, *"Let us create man in our own image."* Ever since that day, the devil has been trying to destroy God's image in man. In the process, he attacks man's self-esteem by telling you and me that *"we are not good enough."* In just a simple Google search you will find that as much as 85% of our population struggles with some element of low self-esteem.

In a survey by the International Coaching Federation, 41% of life coaches reported that low self-esteem is the primary reason for which people seek the professional help of an executive or life coach. This staggering data leads us to ask:

- How do you strengthen your self-esteem?

- How can you help someone struggling with low self-esteem?

Note: The first objective of the Strengths resources is to provide you with a tool to help anyone see that he or she is uniquely created in God's image. Destroying the lies of the devil can help anyone overcome the problem of low self-esteem that infects most of us.

The Need for Work-Life Balance

In the same survey by the International Coaching Federation, 36% of life coaches reported that poor work-life balance is the primary reason for which people seek the professional help of an executive or life coach. Today the majority of urban dwellers work more than 8.5 hours a day. When you factor in commuting time and the time spent working from home the hours devoted to our work-life takes its toll on family life. Also, the average tenure at work is now less than 4.2 years. As a result, people are always looking for that elusive job or what we like to call your sweet spot.

Note: The second objective of the Strengths resources is to provide you with a tool to help people in your life create a process by which they can find their most fulfilling roles. Finding the roles where you can have the greatest impact for God's kingdom is the pathway to fulfilling life callings and achieving more work-life balance.

Application: What Do You Think?

- How does Sam's story reflect the process of change?
- Have you ever tried to help someone change without success? What happened?

- Do you know someone who needs to make some life changes? How can you explain the process of change to him or her?
- What is one thing you wish you could change in your own life? Where are you regarding the process of making change happen?

Tell Jesus

Write a note to Jesus. Summarize the most important things you learned from this section. Tell Him how you wish He would help you. He is sitting right here beside you.

MINISTRY FRAMEWORK

How did Jesus do His ministry? How did He prioritize His time to have such a great impact? How does His model direct how you focus your work, life, and ministry? As we study the attached illustrated framework we will examine:

- How it was represented in the life of Jesus

- How it may relate to your work, life, and ministry

- How the Strengths resources can be used to help you define your roles so you can fulfill your life callings.

VERY IMPORTANT NOTE:

The attached thinking and planning framework can apply to any business or enterprise. In an ideal world, this 3-part jigsaw puzzle would fit perfectly.   Achieving a perfect fit is challenging even in the best-managed organization. In

Christian ministry, this perfect fit is almost impossible because we are imperfect people with imperfect tools and processes. **BUT,** with the presence of Jesus Christ at the center, we can trust Him to bridge the gaps that hinder our imperfect ministries. This is the reason why we call this puzzle a **Christ-centered framework.** With Christ at the center of your life, He will help you define your role. Defining and calibrating your role is the most critical exercise in work-life and ministry. We will briefly describe this framework with more details to follow. Later we will give you a new thinking framework and discussion to help you in defining your roles in life, work, or ministry.

1) It Starts with You

The development framework starts with you, your strengths, and your motivation. **When we look at Jesus as our model,** we see a man who knows His Strengths. At one time He said, *"All authority was given to me."* Matthew 28:15. In his interactions with people, Jesus knew how and where to use his talents. For example, when His mother wanted him to rush into changing the water into wine at the wedding in Cana, He told her this was not the right time in John 2:4. But, motivated by care for his friends, at the right time He acted using His amazing power and talents. In John 14 we see a similar situation in Jesus' response to the death of His friend, Lazarus. While He cared deeply about His friends, He was motivated by a higher and greater purpose that kept him focused on doing the right things at the right time.

What Are Your Strengths?

According to Genesis 1:26, your Strengths are a reflection of God's image in you.   God gave you your Strengths so you can do good work in His kingdom. Based on Matthew 25, you are a steward of your God-given talents and Strengths. If you do not know your Strengths very well, you cannot use them or you may misuse them.   Your most important starting point is to know your Strengths and your identity as one created in God's image.

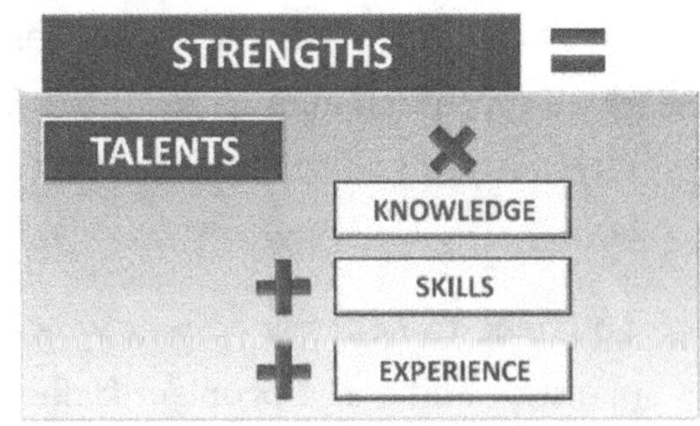

In this self-study resource, **we assume that you have taken the Strengths workshop.**[1] We assume that you understand that your Strengths can be defined using the attached diagram.

- Your Strengths are abilities *"to provide consistent, near-perfect performance in a given activity."*

- Your Strengths start with God-given talents which are revealed in *"naturally recurring patterns of thoughts, feelings or behaviors that can be productively applied."*

> *Making disciples is being intentionally engaged in using your Strengths wherever you may be.*

- Your talents are developed and mature by:
    - The appropriate knowledge you acquire
    - The related skills you develop
    - And the experience of applying your talents, knowledge, skills, and experience to a variety of life situations in a timely and appropriate manner. This is what we call wisdom.[2]

What Are Your Motivations?

Do you wonder what motivated Jesus to come to our world? What motivated Him to go to the Cross? What motivates Him to stay close to you day by day? **It's the engines of purpose and love.**

You need to honestly answer why you want to do this work or ministry. This was a problem facing some of the early church in Corinth. They thought the Lord would be returning soon so they

---

[1] See Appendix for links to Strengths Self Study.
[2] See Appendix for links to Going Deeper in Strengths.

decided to stop working and became idle. This is a temptation and risk into which many of us can easily fall.

Let us start by asking why you get out of bed in the morning. It's your motivation. Why do you bother to eat during the day? It's your motivation. Why do you do anything? It all comes down to motivation. We all have two engines within each of us called motivation. One engine we will call fear; the other we will call love.

The fear motivation drives us to meet **our basic needs** for life and security; beyond that, it does very little. However, the love engine drives us to reflect the image of God. It drives us to do great things for ourselves, our loved ones, our community, and the greater kingdom.   The Bible tells us that, *"God has not given us the spirit of fear but of love, power and a sound mind" 2Timothy 1:7.* "Love motivation" is the power that allows us to make good choices and do great things.

What is Your Purpose?

Jesus knew His purpose and that motivated him for His greatest and toughest roles. Facing His last hours before the cross Jesus said, *"Now my heart is troubled, and what shall I say? 'Father, save me from this hour'? No, it was for this very reason I came to this hour."* (John 12:27) Every engine needs fuel. "Purpose" is the fuel for the love engine. Jack Welsh is one of the most renowned and successful management leaders.   For many years he was the chairman of The General Electric Company (GE). One of his most famous quotes is, **"People work for money but give their life for a purpose."** Pastor Rick Warren's book, *Purpose Driven Life,* sold more than 32 million copies. This book seeks to answer one key question, ***"Why am I here?"*** We all have a basic need to know why we are here.

In one of his video clips on Youtube the Christian comedian, Michael Jr., says that with everything we do, in every role we play we must have a purpose that reflects **"the WHY."** Knowing why we do what we do is what makes what we do more meaningful and impactful. See https://youtu.be/1ytFB8TrkTo

But how do you find purpose? Purpose comes from being with Jesus, to learn from Jesus, and to understand the purpose for which you were created. While many books have been written about purpose, I like to go back to the profound writing of the early church fathers outlined in the "church catechism." It states, **"The chief end of man is to glorify God and enjoy Him forever."** This is a simple and profound truth. It simply tells us we need to look for two things that define our purpose: things that bring glory to God and/or what can help us enjoy Him. C.S. Lewis goes further by saying that, "These are the same thing; fully enjoy is to glorify. In commanding us to glorify Him, God is inviting us to enjoy Him."

The spirit of love gives purpose and power. With this truth, we can join with Paul who says, *"I can do everything through Him [Christ] who gives me strength."* Philippians 4:13.

With a purpose-driven life, now it is up to you. What in the world can you be or do that would bring you great joy and glorify God, your heavenly Father? Answering these questions encourages you to dream and have vision and hope. The Bible tells us that *"without a vision, people perish"*. This applies not only to nations or groups of people but equally to individuals like you and me.

What are Your Passions?

Passions are feelings that can be developed and changed over time. Passions ignite your interests and motivate your curiosity. Unchecked, passions can mislead you. For this reason, they need to be listed and prioritized and harnessed to support your life purpose.

What are the issues that ignite your interests or emotions.? What are you most interested in or curious about? When you look at the many needs and challenges facing your family, your community, your country, or even the world today, what issues make you say "I wish I could…? Where do you see God working and wish you can partner with him to impact the world for Good?

What Rewards Do You Need?

If "purpose" is the fuel that empowers the engine of love, then rewards may be the oil that keeps it running smoothly. God created you and me with a natural need for healthy rewards. At its basic level, rewards come in the form of material compensation for the work or the value we deliver. This kind of compensation needs to be fair and justly paid.   *I Timothy 5:18 tells us "For the Scripture says you shall not muzzle the ox that treads out the corn. And, the laborer is worthy of his reward."*

Beyond meeting fairness and material needs, financial compensation often fades as a good source of healthy rewards. Whether we have financial needs or not, we all need healthy emotional rewards. To discuss this, I wish to leverage the excellent work of Dr. Gary Chapman in his bestseller, *The Five Love Languages.*

Work, ministry, or the demands of family life place emotional demands on our wellbeing. These demands act like withdrawals in our emotional bank account. Those who are important to us are placed by God to make deposits into our emotional bank accounts and build us. Deposits into our emotional bank account come in the form of receiving love. Using the right love language is the best tool for that currency exchange.

The five love languages describe the ways we feel loved and appreciated. Each of us is unique. Depending on our personality we are likely to feel loved differently. Understanding and communicating these differences removes the guesswork and defines clear expectations and needs. To be most effective we need to communicate our love to others in the language of their preference and **not** in our preferred language.

According to Dr. Chapman, there are five love languages: words of affirmation, acts of service, receiving gifts, quality time, and physical touch. We all have these languages but we have our preferences.

1.   **Words of Affirmation:** In this language, you express love with words that build others up. Verbal compliments and words of appreciation do not have to be complicated; the shortest and simplest praises can be the most effective.   Genuine and honest compliments take very little time and effort but go a long way in building our self-esteem and replenishing emotional bank accounts.

2.   **Acts of Service:** Doing things that are helpful and/or kind says that "actions speak louder than words." This is expressed by doing things that you know the other person would like. It does not need to be complicated. It could be cooking a meal, cleaning the house, and picking up a prescription... These often may require some thought, time, and effort. Done with a positive attitude they have a great impact, but doing them out of obligation or with a negative tone should be avoided at all costs.

3.   **Receiving Gifts:** This love language may appear to be materialistic but it is not. Tangible or intangible, gifts are meaningful and thoughtful when they communicate an understanding of the other person's wishes and/or needs. They do not need to be expensive especially when they reflect a generous heart.

4. **Quality Time:** This is giving the gift of time. It says I am here for you and you only. It is all about undivided attention in sharing time or common enjoyable experiences. It is saying you are important enough that I am prepared to put out the rest of the world and focus on your interests, thoughts, and feelings because this means a lot to both of us. In today's busy world, this is a big thing and is a very precious gift.

5.   **Physical Touch:** To people with this love language, nothing is more impactful than the physical touch. Physical touch makes them feel more connected and safer in a world full of challenges and risks. It does not need to be excessive but it must be sincere, timely, appropriate, and not embarrassing.

Identifying the Love Language: Knowing your love language can be one of the single most helpful things in a relationship. To help you and others know your love language Dr. Chapman offers a free online test at http://www.5lovelanguages.com/.   If this is not available to you:

1.   Examine how you show love to others.   This is probably your primary love language.

2.   Watch and observe how the important people in your life express their love to you and others. This is probably their primary love language.

3.   Keep a list of your observations and share them with your important people.

Questions:

- Are you able to simply describe your Strengths to a 12-year-old?

- How do you describe your life purpose to a 12-year-old child?

- How can you help someone discover their God-given Strengths?

2) About Partners and Clients

Going back to the development framework we look at the life of Jesus. He was intentional in reaching out to many people but also focused on those who were ready to change. While He preached to thousands, but He focused on a few who became His partners in ministry. He also prioritized and invested the majority of his time with those who were willing and ready to change. Here we will call them the teachable people or clients.

What Are Their Strengths?

Everyone has something to offer to the kingdom. Regardless of faith, status, or lifestyle, we were all created within the image of God and all have something special and valuable that can contribute to how we see ourselves through the eyes of God.

> *Making disciples is being intentional in in seeing God's image in those He brings our way.*

Regretfully, most often we are tempted to approach others by looking at their needs and what is wrong with them. This blocks our eyes from seeing the grace of God that already exists in them and how God can use what He has already given them. It is always better to start with the strengths God already gave to people even if they do not acknowledge it is God's gift.

Here are some examples:

- God could have very easily taken his people out of Egypt without any human help. But He chose reluctant, stuttering, and fearful Moses. Later He had him use his stick which he turned into a serpent. With that same stick, he had him hit the rock to give them drinking water.

- In calling fishermen like Peter, James, and John, Jesus started by relating to what they knew. He told them He will make them fishers of men.

- In feeding the five thousand, He could have sent manna from heaven. But He used the loaves and fish that were in the hands of a little boy.

- In His teaching, Jesus always started with what people already knew.

We live in a world that has conditioned most of us to believe that we are not good enough. As we stated earlier, as many as 85% of the people you and I meet everyday struggle with self-esteem. The greatest starting point is to help someone see that they have significant value and self-worth. Then you can build on that foundation of self-worth and meet their needs.

Here are two tools that can serve as your ministry starting point if you know people struggling with self-esteem.

- The Bible gives us a clear antidote to the "never good enough virus." In Philippians 4:8 Paul gives us a clear command as he writes, "*Finally, brothers, whatever is true, whatever is noble, whatever is right, whatever is pure, whatever is lovely, whatever is admirable – if anything is excellent or praiseworthy – think about such things.*" Memorizing and obeying this verse could change their world.

- The Strengths self-study resources will help anyone discover their unique talents and cherish them. This resource used the world-renowned StrengthsFinder2.0 assessment from the Gallup Organization. It highlights that everyone is unique. It highlights that the probability of anyone else having the same top 10 strengths in the same order is one in 447 trillion. See https://nomoreoverload.com/home/lys/sss/

What Are Their Needs?

While Jesus had all authority and power, in his encounter with people he focused on their most pressing needs. When He met the man who was lying at the pool of Bethesda, He did not preach to him about the Kingdom of heaven or the forgiveness of sin. Instead, He healed him. The same with the woman who was caught in adultery; He did not remind her of the commandments but rather He granted her what she needed most, mercy.

As I am writing these notes our country, indeed the whole world is in the grip of a pandemic. The coronavirus is on

> *Making disciples is being intentionally engaged in meeting needs.*

everyone's mind. While back pain, cancer, and heart disease are critical issues, our healthcare resources are focused on dealing with this very obvious priority that will impact the vast majority of our world.

Similarly, while many needs demand our attention and provide ministry opportunities, we have one pressing human ailment. It is separation from God and the need for a personal relationship through Jesus Christ.   While this disease is not visible, its symptoms may be easily visible. To summarize, even **at the risk of repeating myself,** allow me to highlight two that the Strengths workshop seeks to address:

1. **The need for self-esteem.** As referenced earlier, surveys indicate that as many as 85% of us struggle with some kind of low self-esteem. In a survey by the International Federation of Coaches, 41% of life coaches reported that low self-esteem is the primary reason for which people seek the professional help of an executive or life coach.

2. **The need for work-life balance:** In the same survey by the International Federation of Coaches, 36% of life coaches reported that work-life balance is the primary reason for which people seek the professional help of an executive or life coach. The ambiguity of roles and lack of self-esteem drives most of us to work longer hours in a very stress-filled environment. In the process, we compromise sleep, health, and family life.

The Strengths workshop resources are designed to help a person:

1. Discover his unique strengths as a reflection of God's image. This could be the most powerful antidote to the problem of low self-esteem.

2. Create a process to define roles and relationships and find the sweet-spot in work, life, and ministry. This could lead to improved work-life balance.

3- About Processes and Tools

Let's go back to the development framework highlighting **processes.** Since the beginning of creation, we see that God is a process-oriented Creator. In the six-day creation story, we see an orderly way of creating things in a sequence where one part of creation supported the next.

In His life and ministry, we see Jesus being very intentional and systematic in many ways. Before starting His ministry, He took 40 days alone with His father. I do not doubt that these were planning and preparation days. This was followed by the fulfillment of His prophetic appointment from John the Baptist.

> *Making disciples is being intentional in using our time, talents, and material treasures.*

Although He had authority and power to do anything, we see a well-organized process-oriented leader through His encounters with those He taught, healed, and fed. In sending out the disciples two by two to preach into the neighboring villages He gave them a very clear process with step by step instructions of what to do if their message was accepted and contingencies if they were rejected.

Regarding tools, we see God using dust to create Adam and then using one of His ribs to create Eve. Later, during His ministry, Jesus used many different tools to communicate His message and fulfill His roles. For example, we see Him using some old jars and water to create wine, using mud to open the eyes of a blind man, using a few loaves to feed more than five thousand people. Jesus was a master at using stories and illustrations to engage His audience and communicate His truth.

Throughout all of His ministry, Jesus was very intentional in reaching out to the many but also focused on those who were ready to change. While He preached to thousands, he invested the majority of his time with very few. This is the model we tried to follow as we structured the tools and processes of the Strengths Resources.

The Strengths Resources are a collection of **five tools and processes** that we hope you can use as you seek to make disciples and fulfill His great commission. Just as in the days of Jesus, while the majority of people have two common needs and can benefit from what you have to share with them, their willingness to invest the time and commitment will vary greatly. To optimize the use of your ministry resources and respond to their need at the point of their commitment we encourage you to view the Strengths resources in two categories:

- **Starting with Outreach Tools and Processes:**
    1. **How Are You Card and Wellness Gauge** could be tools to help you reach out and engage with people at an initial level. [3]
    2. **The Strengths Self-Study** may be the answer for self-motivated individuals who wish to have total control of the learning process. [4]
    3. **The Strengths Video Workshop** could be an ideal resource for people who are curious or believe they need help and are willing to invest a half-day in a facilitated workshop setting.[5]

- **Discipleship and Leadership Development Tools and Processes:**

---

[3] See Appendix for links to How Are You Card and Wellness Gauge

[4] See Appendix for links to Strengths Self Study Tool Set.

[5] See Appendix for links to Strengths Video Workshop.

- o **The Strengths Learning Lab** is a structured relationship-building toolset. It uses a well-established Bible study format as well as the emerging "Flipped Classroom" model.[6]

- o **Strengths Development Coaching** is for those who are seeking help in the area of self-esteem, work-life balance, and/or job change. For those who are passionate about using Strengths in the process of making disciples we seek to offer a structured toolset based on what we call "Christ-centered coaching."

4) About Jesus

In the Development Framework Diagram, we see Jesus as the link that ties the other three parts of the diagram together.   Without Him, everything falls apart.

> *Making disciples is being intentional in "being with Jesus to learn from Jesus how to become like Jesus."*

The diagram illustrates that making disciples is **being** with Jesus to **learn** from Jesus to **become** like Jesus and **act** like Jesus. Disciple-making is all about JESUS. Fortunately, after giving us the great commission He said, "*I am with you always, even unto the end of the world.*" Let us examine how His promise relates to this illustrated framework.

Jesus and You

Examining your Strengths and motivation:

- Regardless of how much you try to learn about your talents, you will never fully understand them the way He does.

- Regardless of how much knowledge you seek to acquire, you will never know enough.

---

[6] See Appendix for links for Links to Strengths Learning Lab.

- Regardless of all the skills you may develop, you will never be good enough for all the challenges life brings.
- Regardless of how much experience you gain, your wisdom will always be imperfect.
- Regardless of how hard you try, deep within your heart, you will always be imperfect.

What does this mean? You need Him to fill-in all your shortcomings and He can do this because:

- He created you in His perfect image and understands your potential.
- He is all-knowing and all-wise and promised to give wisdom when we ask.
- He can create in you a clean heart and pure motives.

Jesus and Others

Examining their Strengths and needs:

- Regardless of how much you can learn about their talents and Strengths, you are still an outsider; you will never fully know them or their potential.
- While they may try to express their needs, you can never uncover their hidden secrets and concerns or fully understand their cares and challenges.

What does this mean? You need Him to bridge the gap and help you communicate based on His perfect knowledge and love for those He brings your way.

Jesus and Processes and Tools:

He is the all resourceful one.

- All the tools we can give you are all man-made and imperfect at best.

- All the processes that we envision and the plans we make are all limited by our finite understanding and our limitations.
- Our abilities to apply even the best processes and tools are limited and hindered by our imperfect being.

What does this mean? You and I need Him to bridge the gap created by our imperfections.

Application: What can you do?

Jesus gave us a two-part command:

- *"Remain in Me, and I will remain in you. No branch can bear fruit by itself." Jesus said, 'I am the vine; you are the branches. If a man remains in Me and I in him, he will bear much fruit; apart from Me, you can do nothing.' " John 15:4-6*
- *"If you remain in Me and My words remain in you, ask whatever you wish, and it will be given you. This is to my Father's glory, that you bear much fruit, showing yourselves to be My disciples." John 15: 8*

If you and I are truly grafted into Him, He will give you a vision and power. The Bible says that without a vision you and I will atrophy and even perish. Your vision starts by having an energizing purpose that is aligned with His purpose for the world.

Jesus is calling you to partner with him so that *"His Kingdom may come on earth as it is in heaven"*. Pastor Steve Shaw is quoted saying, *"God's Kingdom and God's will are the same things. God's will is to restore God's world through God's people in God's time."* He is calling you to be His co-laborer in this amazing process of restoring His world.   Can you think of anything more exciting? If this is your vision start thinking of the roles you can play.

Tell Jesus

Write a note to Jesus asking His help as you apply this framework to your life or ministry.

DEFINING ROLES

The role Jesus gives you to play has a dual purpose. The first and most important purpose **is your development.** The second is that you may lead others so they can be with Him and learn from Him.

You and I have a stewardship responsibility and are given talents and Strengths to share what we have learned from Him as He instructed us in Matthew 28. In doing so we must be very clear about the role He is calling you to play.

Defining clear roles is a critical part of any effective organization.[7] In defining a role, we seek to apply the **5 key points** illustrated in the attached diagram. Here we will reference each of these examining the general role of **"leader."** Later we will highlight specific distinctive of the role you may play while using the five different Strengths Resources we referenced earlier.

> *Making disciples is being intentional defining your roles.*

You as a Leader

Jesus calls you to be his co-laborer not so much because He needs you, but rather because He can enjoy your fellowship and desires to help you become more like himself. Further, this role is a great opportunity to help you grow in knowing yourself and others but most importantly in knowing Jesus Christ himself.

---

[7] See Appendix for links to Roles Template.

FOUNDATIONS

As a co-laborer with Christ, you are a co-leader with Christ. Jesus demonstrated His leadership in the many roles he played. We will discuss a general framework for defining what we mean by a co-leader with Jesus. Later we will narrow that definition and relate it to the 5 Strengths resources. Then we will discuss the use of the roles of:

1. **Listener,** by using the "How Are You Card" and "Wellness Gauge"

2. **An encourager,** by using the Strengths Self Study tools

3. **An Organizer,** by using the Strengths Video Workshop

4. **A Facilitator,** by using the Strengths Learning Lab

5. **A Coach**, by using the Strengths Development Tools.

In each of these roles, we will highlight that our ultimate purpose is to use Strengths development as a tool for drawing people into a personal relationship with the One who gave them their strengths.

Three key factors contribute to successful leadership of any kind:

*   **Faithfulness:** Being faithful to Jesus as your primary leader and your foundational source of power.   In addition, you must be faithful to what you believe about the application of Strengths in your own life. Finally, faithfulness is seen in your relationships with those you lead by communicating transparency and integrity.

*   **Teachable:** This is the hallmark of good leaders. The primary purpose is your personal development. Continually seek input from Jesus and others. This will help you grow in your understanding of yourself, the application of the Strengths material, and appreciation of those you seek to lead.

*   **Commitment:** Commitment is revealed in availability and the time you invest. Without the investment of time, you can never be faithful or teachable.

Your Strengths

In Matthew 25 Jesus gave a very powerful parable called the parable of the talents. Based on this parable, you and I are accountable for knowing our talents and using them wisely. We assume that you have taken

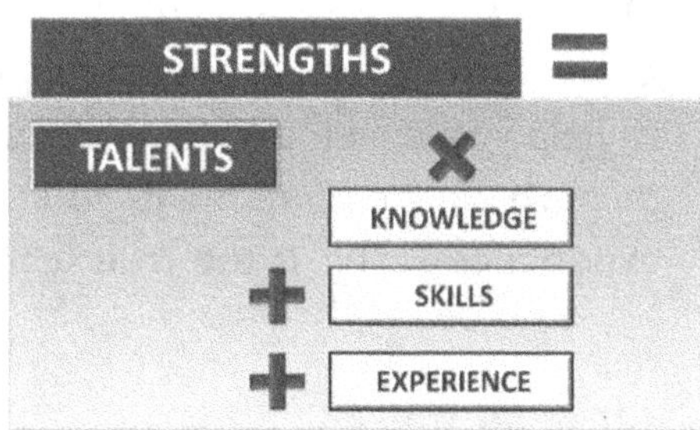

the Strengths training and that you understand that your Strengths start with God-given talents and mature through the attached diagram and formula.

Some may ask what strengths are needed to succeed. Your specific strengths do not define the role, rather they define:

- How you are likely to play the role
- What responsibilities of the role you need to prioritize
- What aspects of the role you need to delegate to others.

Later we will give more input to the application of the Strengths formula and your role in using the various parts of the Strengths Resources. The parts of the illustrated formula are:

- **Talents:** One of the best ways to describe talents is by using adjectives. We encourage you to think of the key adjectives that best describe you.
- **Knowledge:** In developing these resources we tried to reduce the required knowledge to a minimum. Having said that, two critical areas are mandatory:
    - A growing understanding of self-identity in Jesus. This comes from a visible commitment to **"Being with Jesus to learn from Jesus to become like Jesus."**
    - A good and understanding of your Strengths profile having taken the Living Your Strengths Workshop and/or the Strengths Self-Study tools set.
- **Skills:** Skills are the steps to the application of knowledge. This resource is intended to help you develop the skills you need. Later we will provide guidelines to help you develop the skills required for the roles related to the Strengths

resources. We will also help you learn that the two most important leadership skills are the skill of active listening and the skill of asking good and engaging questions.

- **Experience:** The Strengths resources are provided as a tool to help you develop your experience. We believe that through your commitment, you will gain experience upon experience. This is the true school of life.

Your People

Your roles are all about relationships. This is a great opportunity for your life to be impacted by people and for you to impact the lives of other people. Here we will discuss two types of people.

Important People - Partners

If you plan to do something significant for Christ, it is only natural to expect that the Devil will seek to obstruct you or even destroy you. Ministry is a dangerous place for those who want to do it alone. Ecclesiastes 4:12 highlights the importance of relationships in ministry. *"By yourself, you're unprotected. With a friend, you can face the worst. Can you round up a third? A three-stranded rope isn't easily snapped."* The Message. In addition to the Lord Jesus, along your side, you need important people. **The important people are your partners in your life, work or ministry.** They support you, collaborate with you, and or oversee and protect you.

About the Overseer

Let us talk more about the role of your overseer. The overseer is entrusted with an awesome privilege and responsibility. While some may think that the primary responsibility of the overseer is finding the right workers, developing those God instructs into His care is far greater and more critical. No role, organization, or ministry should exist without an intentionally responsible overseer.

Jesus highlights the most important role of the overseer in His conversation with Peter in John 15:15-17 *"When they had finished eating, Jesus said to Simon Peter, 'Simon son of John, do you truly love me more than these?' 'Yes, Lord,' he said, 'you know that I love you.' Jesus said, 'Feed my lambs.' Again, Jesus said, 'Simon son of John, do you truly love me?' He answered, 'Yes, Lord, you know that I love you.' Jesus said, 'Take care of my sheep.' The third time he said to him, 'Simon son of John, do you love me?' Peter was hurt because Jesus asked him the third time, 'Do you love me?' He said, 'Lord, you know all things; you know that I love you.' Jesus said, 'Feed my sheep'."* While recruiting and administration may be important, the primary responsibility of the overseer is shepherding and developing those he or she is entrusted to oversee.

If you are called to be an overseer here is what may be considered a basic action plan or responsibility:

- **Pray.** Pray for each **person you oversee** by name weekly. As you pray, ask the Lord to reveal to you what you should do for His precious sheep.
- **Connect:** Once a week contact your team by phone, mail, and text. Be an encourager.
- **Meet:** At least once a month meet individually with your people to assess how they are doing physically, emotionally, spiritually, and relating to work-life issues. You may wish to use the wellness gauge tools.
- **Observe:** Attend appropriate event or activities to support and encourage those you oversee:
    - **Encouragement:** Ask God to lead you to some positive attributes, observations, or results that you can share with others.

- o **Instructions:** Seek ways to help develop the skills of those you oversee.
- o **Evaluate:** Meet to evaluate the effectiveness of this ministry.
- o **Report:** Communicate as expected by the church leadership that is the God-given authority over your role.

Teachable people - Clients

The purpose is to draw people into a closer relationship with Jesus. **The teachable people are the clients or the beneficiaries of the role you are called to play.** There are many ways teachable people will be introduced to your ministry:

- **Promotion and advertising:** These are the traditional and least effective way.
- **Personal Invitation:** This is by far the most effective way. Following the model of Jesus, we see that He invited others to join Him. Prompted by the Holy Spirit, you and your partners should be encouraged to invite others on the journey. This invitation process should include all those interested in helping people on the discipleship pathway.

Your Responsibilities

When we look at the conversation between Jesus and Peter, we see three key possible areas of responsibilities. They are shepherding, outcome, and results, as well as administration.

Shepherding

This is your opportunity to build one on one relationship for greater impact. You are a shepherd of those God will entrust into this unique relationship. This involves effort, time, and sensitivity to the Holy Spirit. In John 10:14 Jesus provides a picture that best describes the relationship between the shepherd and the sheep *"I am the good shepherd; I know my sheep and my sheep know me."* Jesus is the good shepherd and He is calling you to partner with Him so you would know those He entrusts into your care.

Outcome and Results

This is about delivering some measurable results. This is the area where your preparation and dependence on the Lord are engaged for a great impact on those God entrusts into your care and where you will use tools and processes to deliver the right objectives of your ministry.   We will discuss this in more detail later.

Administration

The Strengths Ministry is designed to require minimum administration. All the resources you need are provided in a simple, easy to access way. The lessons are practical and can be self-taught through the self-study web-based resources.

About Measurements and Indicators

It has been said that we measure what we value.   The Lord of the harvest expects us to be intentional in measuring what we can measure and leaving what we cannot measure to His infinite wisdom.   I suggest there are three areas of measurements that we may consider:

- **Shepherding:** Loving people. This is a most important measurement or key performance indicator given to us by Jesus in *John 13:34-35 "A new commandment I give unto you, that ye love one another; as I have loved you, that ye also love one another. By this shall all men know that ye are my disciples if ye* *have love one to another.".* Please note that this is the ONLY new commandment that Jesus gave.

- **Outcome:** In *John 21:17* when Jesus tells Peter to *"Feed my sheep"* He is not calling for just protection and survival. The results of good shepherding are revealed in growth. In addition to measuring the learning outcome, the Lord is interested in how you are growing to become more like Him and how you enhance your leadership skills.

- **Organizational:** You are entrusted with the time given to you by others. This is revealed by how you manage the time and how engaged each member feels about their participation in your ministry.

About Surveys:

Simple surveys can be an effective tool to provide some basic measurement indicators. It is important to make the survey confidential and anonymous. Using a few subjective and qualitative statements that reflect how your group members feel, such a survey requires little time and administration. Further, this input can be easily summarized using a simple Excel sheet.

About Ministry Term

Ministry should never be a life sentence. While the preference is for a longer-term commitment, the ministry term should be limited to a specific period with the option of being renewed as the Lord directs. Naturally, this renewal should be confirmed by the agreement of the overseer.

Empowerment

Empowerment is revealed in the following three dimensions:

- **Authority:** Authority is permission to play the assigned role. God created authority and structure for the protection of His people and His kingdom. The church was established by Jesus as an expression of a Biblical structure.

Imperfect in its human components, it is still the most appropriate structure for the application of the Strengths ministry.

- **Resources:** By God's grace and provision of the internet all the needed resources are provided to you free of charge other than those required by third party organizations.

- **Time:** This is the time that we must commit to this ministry. In Romans 12:1 Paul admonishes us to *"Present our bodies as a living sacrifice."* This can be reflected in giving our talents and Strengths into the service of God's kingdom. Later we will seek to provide some guidelines regarding the amount of time required for each area of ministry.

Application: What can you do?

Allow me to share something I believe from my personal experience. Through the past 50 plus years, I have worked for more than 12 corporations and served more than 2,000 clients. Most of my 30 years in the corporate world were involved in the application of new technologies in the process of change management. During the past 20 plus years of our consulting and coaching practice, we had the privilege of personal communication with hundreds of clients from all walks of life.

Based on this, we can say that ill-defined and miscommunicated roles are the greatest causes leading to stress and overload in both work and ministry. We hope that this simple tool can help you avoid such critical pitfalls.

Tell Jesus

Write a note to Jesus. Tell Him what you think of your roles and what changes you wish to make. Ask Him to help you. He is willing and able.

STRENGTHS RESOURCES AND TOOLS

OVERVIEW

The five Strengths Ministry
resources are placed in two
categories. The outreach tools
require limited time and effort but
the two discipleship and leadership
development tools will require

> *Making disciples is being intentional in the proper use of whatever tools and processes God provides.*

commitment and significant time investment. Following this brief
overview, we will give you more detail on each of these tools. We
will use true stories:

- To discuss how you may apply them using the development
  framework we referenced earlier and

- To help you define the role you can play using them guided by
  the development framework we discussed in the first part of
  this book.

Outreach Tools:

- **The How Are You Card.** This, along with the associated
  Wellness Gauge, are tools to help you reach out and engage
  with people as a friend. With this, we will discuss the role of **a
  listener.**

- **Strengths Self-Study** may be the answer for self-motivated
  individuals who wish to have total control of the learning
  process; with this, we will discuss the role of an **encourager.**

- **Strengths Video Workshop** could be an ideal resource for
  people who are curious or believe they need help and are
  willing to invest a half-day in a facilitated workshop setting.
  With this, we will discuss the role of an Organizer.

Discipleship and Leadership Development Tools

- **The Strengths Learning Lab** is a structured relationship-building toolset. It uses a well-established Bible study format as well as the emerging "Flipped Classroom" model https://nomoreoverload.com/home/lys/sll/. With this, we will discuss the role of a **facilitator**.

- **Strengths Development Coaching** is for those who are seeking help in the area of self-esteem or work-life balance. For those who are passionate about using Strengths in the process of making disciples we seek to offer a structured toolset based on what we call "Christ-centered coaching" https://nomoreoverload.com/home/lys/sdc/ccc/. With this, we will discuss the role of a Coach.

THE HOW ARE YOU CARD

Playing the Role of a listener.

You meet someone in the church, a family gathering, or even at work. What do you often say? Most likely the most common greeting is, **"How are you?"** Most likely you will get the very common response, "Fine, thank you." The disciple-making conversation needs to go far deeper. So how do we do it?

Meeting Tom Wang

The airport in Bogota, Colombia was very busy. Going through security was much slower than I expected. My flight had begun boarding as I prayed, "Lord, I want to go home; please don't let me miss my flight." As I ran towards the gate, I thought I was going to be the last one on the plane. Throwing myself into seat 7C, I noticed that the two seats beside me were empty.   I thanked the Lord that I would have some extra room to stretch and have a nap during this long flight.

Just as the gate was about to close, a tough-looking man appeared and headed towards me. Pointing at the empty window seat he bellowed, *"This is my seat"*. He looked tough and unfriendly so I decided to keep quiet.   It is amazing how quickly we size up people and give them labels that define how we communicate with them. Just as the plane began to take off, I looked at him he was already fast asleep.

Two hours later the flight attendants woke him up to hand him his dinner tray. He looked at it and said, *"I hate airplane food. I do not know how any human can eat this stuff."* Noticing that I had already started to devour my food, he apologized, *"I am sorry, I am in the fine food business so I tend to be a bit picky."* *"No, problem"*, I replied. I commented, *"You look tired. How are you?"* He quickly replied, *"I am fine. Just working long hours and needed a bit of sleep."*

Looking at him I said, *"I am Baha."* He quickly reached his hand and with a firm grip he said, *"I am Tom, Tom Wang." "What kind of work do you do?"* I asked. This simple question started an hour-long conversation. It was mostly a one-sided talk.   He talked and I listened.   Occasionally I nodded or asked for some explanation to assure him that I was interested and listening. He told me about the three restaurants he had in Toronto and the new high-end Korean Grill he was opening in Bogota.

He talked about the challenges of hiring the right staff and making sure he had the right talent on his team. With this, I asked him if he had the right tool to select talent and if he knew about StrengthsFinder2.0. To my surprise, he did. He had the book on his phone. He knew much more about Strengths than I expected. He thanked me for giving him the idea to let all his staff do the Strengths assessment. He took note of our workshop and was pleased that we had a free workshop in Spanish.

WOW, I thought to myself. I truly misjudged him. He was much more talkative and friendly than I initially expected him to be. After about an hour of talking, I felt the Lord leading me to see if I can move the conversation to a different level. I prayed for wisdom.

Reaching into my wallet I pulled out my **"How Are You Card"**. (See the attached image.[8])

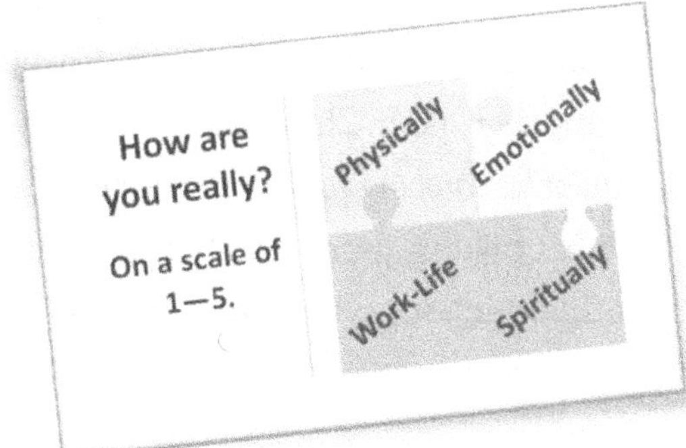

Looking at him I said, *"Tom, you are a very gracious man. You drive yourself hard to accomplish a lot in your life. And by most standards, you are very successful. When I asked you how you are, you answered that you were fine. But what does that mean? How do you measure "fine"?*

I have this little card that I use with my friends. I call it my "How Are You Gauge". Would you mind if show it to you? With a curious look, he responded, *"Sure."*

As I gave him the card, I said, *"This card has 4 parts of an integrated jigsaw puzzle. It asks the question on a scale of 1 – 5 how you are doing and specifically how are you physically, emotionally, spiritually, and concerning work-life issues."* As we talked about each of the four parts of the card, he opened up and spoke more freely than I even expected. I said VERY little until we came to the "How are you spiritually?"   He seemed a bit hesitant so I asked, *"How are you spiritually?"* He replied, *"I do not know; I am not sure I know how to answer this."*

At this point, I asked his permission if I could tell him where I stood in my relationship with Jesus. Before he could say no, I told

---

[8] See Appendix for links to download How Are You Card.

him very briefly about my relationship as a follower of Jesus and how this impacts my self-identity and life priorities physically, emotionally, spiritually, and in all aspects of my work life.

He replied by telling me that he grew up in a non-practicing Buddhist family but went to the Catholic school system because his mother liked Christians. Then he said, "*I guess you can say that I am still searching for what I believe.*" With this, he changed the subject talking about his children and why he put them in the Catholic school system only as a follow up to what his mother did with him.

Then he asked if he could keep the "How are You card". He said "*I would like to use it with my daughter; I will have dinner with her tomorrow. This could be quite helpful. She always tells me she is fine but I think she is not telling me the truth.   She is closer to her mother; this may open up our conversation quite a bit.*" With this, I felt it was time to take the conversation in a different direction by talking about his two sons and their work, sports, and Strengths.

As we were ready to land in Toronto, I gave Tom my business card saying, "*If you ever want to talk more, please let me know.*" As he gave me another very firm handshake, he said ***"Thank you very much; I really enjoyed our conversation. I will always remember what you said and I hope we can meet again."***

As I reflect on our two-hour conversation, Tom spoke for almost 90% of the time.   Except for the brief explanation of my faith and relationship with Jesus, I said very little and asked a few questions. I wondered what role I played.

As we parted with Tom, I thought to myself, "*Lord, I said very little; where do I fit in the process of changing this man's life into the disciple you wish for him to be?*' God did not answer, as if He were telling me, "*That is not your business.*"

The Story Behind the Card.

There is a simple story behind this simple "How are You card." Arriving home from work one day my wife and children greeted me with warm affection. My wife looked at me and said, "How are you?" I gave the customary reply, "I'm fine." She said "You do not look it," Irritated, I replied, **"I TOLD YOU I'M FINE**." I am sure you can guess the rest of the conversation. You probably can guess what the dinnertime looked like and the kind of conversations my wife and I had that evening.

How are you?" We all say it but what does it mean? What should be our response? This was the challenge my wife and I faced in our very busy lives. Since we were committed to honest communication we used to ask, *"How are you really, on a scale of 1-5?"* Over the years, this developed into this simple, business card size conversation tool that we share with friends and clients. Many of our friends have started using it with their friends and family.   We hope you do as well.

To help our clients this simple card evolved into another tool that I use with those who are interested in going further in this dialog or conversation. This is a tool we call **"The Wellness Gauge."** It is a confidential web-based assessment. We simply send the link to the interested party so they can do this 4-minute test. In return, the system will email them a personalized confidential 2-page report.   Should he or she wish to talk about it further, we will meet where we can discuss observations, desired change, and how I may be able to help.

More about the use of this tool when we discuss Strengths Coaching. For now, we offer you the chance to try it for yourself. Go to https://nomoreoverload.com/home/lys/sdc/wg/ and use the code **"GUEST."**

What Do Listeners Do?

Listeners listen. This may sound too simple, but regretfully, it is VERY hard. Effective listening is an amazing skill. God is a perfect listener. Just consider how much He listens to you and me. Sadly, most of us feel that we need to talk to add value to the conversation. We need to defend our views and protect our vulnerable self-esteem. According to Proverbs, the opposite is true. *"A truly wise person uses few words; a person with understanding is even-tempered."* (Proverbs 17:27-28 NLT) If I tried to put this proverb into modern language I may say, *"A truly wise man practices effective listening."*

> *In his book, Just Listen, psychologist and author, Dr. Mark Goulston, says that "People do not change because of what you say, rather, much more because of what you get them to say."*

Effective listing is a skill that would serve any of us in all of life's circumstances. There are many corporate and academic courses on how to develop this vital skill. Searching amazon.com I found 752 books on the subject. Seeking to become an effective listener is a journey.

To get you started, here is a simple definition. **An effective listener** seeks to understand more than to be understood. He or she listens actively to what is being said, displays a genuine interest in the topic but more importantly in the person speaking, provides feedback, and asks good pertinent questions; so, the speaker knows that he or she is clearly understood.

Psychologist, Raychelle C. Lohmann, suggests that good listeners share these characteristics:

- *They pay attention to the person who is speaking.*

- *They keep eye contact.*

- *They show interest by nodding or smiling at appropriate times.*

- *They make sure that they understand what has been said by repeating it in their own words. For example, a good listener might say, "Do you mean that ...?"*

- *They let the other person finish his or her thoughts without interrupting.*

- *They ask questions if anything is not clear when the speaker has finished.*

1) YOUR:
- Strengths
- Motivations
- Rewards

2) PARTNERS & CLIENTS
- Strengths
- Opportunities
- Needs

JESUS

3) TOOLS AND PROCESS
- PARTNERS: Connection and Engagement
- CLIENTS: Service and Delivery

I know you may be too busy to engage in a long course on active or effective listening. Should you have some time, watch these short Ted Talks and YouTube clips:

- https://www.youtube.com/watch?v=IwWj_SfDpzg

- https://www.youtube.com/watch?v=iWPkHHIchIE

- https://www.youtube.com/watch?v=A343tIP5iUA

- https://www.youtube.com/watch?v=saXfavoIOQo

- https://youtu.be/Yq5pJ0q3xuc

When you are done with that, take time and look for some short articles on effective listening or how to become an effective listener. Remember, this is an important skill that will serve you in all aspects of your life.

Exercise: What Can You do?

Going back to the description of the ministry framework we provided earlier, picture yourself in an encounter similar to the one I had with Tom Wang. How can you modify my experience and adapt it to your world so you can also similarly help others? If possible, ask God to bring to your mind a specific person. For ease of description let us call this person Joe.   For an exercise try to answer the following questions:

- **About you: What Strengths and Motivation?**
    - o   What natural talents? Use adjectives to describe them.
    - o   What Knowledge + Skill + Experience will help you relate to Joe?
    - o   What are your motivations? Why would you wish to help Joe?
- **About your Joe:** What Strengths (Talents X Knowledge + Skills + Experience) has he been given? What are his needs or life challenges?
- **About tools and processes:** Think of:
    - o   **Connecting tools and processes.** What can you do to connect with people like Joe? How can you use the "How are You card" or the Wellness Gauge as effective tools?
    - o   **Serving tools and processes:** How can you use the "How are You card" or the Wellness Gauge? Remember these are tools to be adapted to your style and need.

I am glad God gave me this little "How are you card". It has proven to be a very flexible little tool that I have used with close family members, business clients, and even total strangers. Over the years I have learned that what most people crave is finding a good listener.

- **About Jesus:** Remember, there is never a perfect fit. Jesus will fill in the gaps. He is more than able. How would you like to ask Him to help you so you can help your Joe?

Although I have not heard from Tom Wang since that day, I know Jesus is not finished with him yet. Just like the teacher in his Catholic school, I am just a step in the process of pointing him to Jesus.

More About Delivery Process

You may wonder how this "How are You card" relates to Strengths. This is a simple conversation starter tool. It is presented as a 4-part jigsaw puzzle. We know that God created us in His image and His desire is for all parts of the card to fit together and work together in harmony. The jigsaw puzzle serves to illustrate this:

- **Spiritually:** Knowing our Strengths as a reflection of God's image is at the center of our relationship with Him and how we feel spiritually.

- **Emotionally:** God desires for us to work in harmony with one another. Knowing our Strengths and the Strengths of others impacts how we communicate and collaborate with others as well as what restores or drains us emotionally.

- **Physically:** The Bible says that our bodies are "the temple of the Holy Spirit". Playing to our Strengths energizes us.

- **Work-life:** Most of us spend a large percentage of our time at work. Surveys by the Gallup Organization indicate that *"People who use their strengths every day are three times more likely to report having an excellent quality of life, six times more likely to be engaged at work, 8% more productive and 15% less likely to quit their jobs. Regretfully* **ONLY** *17% of those surveyed globally, use their Strengths every day."* Defining our work roles in harmony with our Strengths enhances productivity, profitability as well as corporate well-being.

How does this work in real life? The process hinges on asking open-ended questions, listening well, and waiting for the opportunity to engage about the importance of "living your Strengths". There are many ways to do this. It could start with simple questions like:

- Would you like to improve some of these scores?

- What do you think of this? Data provided by Gallup suggests that *"people who use their strengths every day are 3 times more likely to report having an excellent quality of life."*

> a. Do you use your Strengths every day?
>
> b. Would you like to discover your Strengths?

- **OR** Would you like to do a free self-assessment that gives you more detail on each of the four parts of the jigsaw puzzle? If you wish, we could meet and talk about the report that you will get.

Exercise: What is Your Role?

Jesus said, "I am with you always." With this in view, in any encounter, I stop and ask His input. *How do I do this?* I simply take a moment and ask, *"Lord what role do you want me to play here?"* To answer this question, I follow the process outlined earlier in the section on roles and illustrated in the attached diagram.

Through my encounter with Tom Wang, I could have played many roles. But as I prayed, I sensed the Lord telling me, **"Be a listener."** This seems to be the most common role I get to play in the first stage of all relationships. This is especially true when I have used my "How are You card" or "the Wellness Gauge." In our very busy lives, being a listener is one of the most cherished roles. It is one of the most valuable roles. Think of

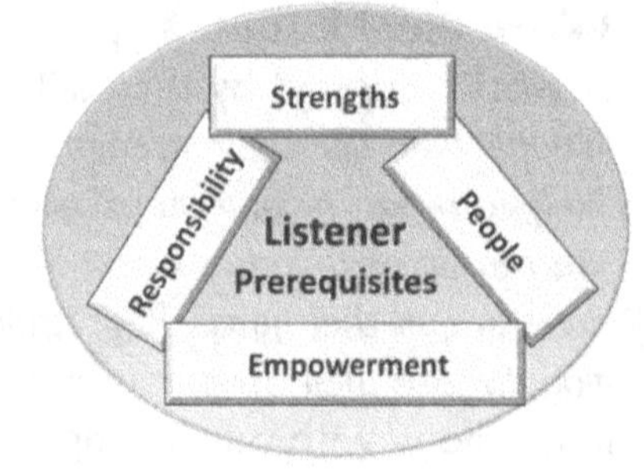

how often God plays this role in your life and mine. Be like Him. Just listen!

With the Holy Spirit as your partner, consider the following. If you were in a similar place with your friend, Joe, what role would you play? How would you define your role? Consider the following questions related to the attached diagram:

- **Listener prerequisite:** what are the prerequisite qualifications for this role?

- **What strengths** do you bring to this role?
    - o   Natural Talents? Use adjectives to describe them.
    - o   Knowledge + skills + experience. List the most likely that could relate to Joe.
- **Who are the important and teachable people** in your role?
    - o   Who are the partners who will support you?
    - o   Who are the teachable people? What are their Strengths and needs?
- **What responsibilities** do you have? What are you accountable for?
- **What empowerment** do you need? Be sure to consider tools and resources as well as how much time you are prepared to invest or spend with Joe.

Tell Jesus

- Go back and examine the thoughts shared in this section.
- Journal and summarize your observations. Write them down.
- Share what you learned as a written conversation with Jesus. Remember, He is listening and He said, "I am with you always."

Tell Jesus what you would like to do as a result of what you have learned. Tell Him how you want Him to help you.

STRENGTHS SELF-STUDY

Playing the Role of Encourager

What do you do when your professional life falls apart and you feel that you have nothing else to live for? Even when you expect it, life can be very tough, especially when you have no plan.

Samira knew that this day would eventually come but hoped it will be delayed for as long as possible. In her busy life, she never planned for what would happen when this day would arrive. The university where she worked had become her extended family. It was the place where she studied and where she had her job for the last 32 years. Since she did not have any children, her career had become her source of self-identity. Now she could be facing mandatory retirement at age 60.

The Administration Director where Samira worked often had given her hope that because of her skills and talents he could bend the policies and delay her mandatory retirement date to a much later age. But then the day came when her director invited her into his office to tell her the bad news.

Although she was a close family member, our conversations were often shallow. This time was different. I could sense that things were not OK. The 9,000 kilometers that separated us could not hide her pain. I could tell she could not hold back the tears and the quivers in her voice. I said, "Lord, can I help such a precious woman?" We live in two different cultures and any advice I may give her will most likely be based on my flawed understanding and assumptions.

There were three unshakable truths that I could count on:

- The first is that God loved her and cared about her pain and her future.

- The second is that God had given Samira many Strengths (talents, knowledge, + skills + experience) that she could use to build a new future. My job was to help her find a way to discover her Strengths that could relate to her new life circumstances.

- Over the following few weeks, I had several conversations with Samira. In most of them, I played the role of listener. Most often they started by "How are you?" or "How are you really?" How are you on a scale of 1-5…?

When the time was right, I asked her if she would like to invest the time in a self-study course that would help her discover her true talents and possibly find a new career. *"Of course, I would,"* she quickly replied. At this time I pointed her to the Strengths Self-Study tools. Over the following weeks, I kept in touch with Samira as my role changed from a listener to an encourager and a point of accountability.

What Do Encouragers Do?

We admire the people in the first church as outlined in Acts and the letters of the apostles. Why? Because of their faith? Yes? Because of their perseverance? Yes, but also for the kind of relationships they had with each other. The role of an encourager played a very vital part in the life of the early church.

- Acts 15:32: *"Judas and Silas, who themselves were prophets, said much to encourage and strengthen the brothers."*

- Romans 12:8: "if it is encouraging, let him encourage;"

- Colossians 4:8: *"I am sending him to you for the express purpose that you may know about our circumstances and that he may encourage your hearts."*

- I Thessalonians 3:2: *"We sent Timothy, who is our brother and God's fellow-worker in spreading the gospel of Christ, to strengthen and encourage you in your faith,"*

- I Thessalonians 4:18: *"Therefore encourage each other."*

- I Thessalonians 5:11: *"Therefore encourage one another and build each other up, just as in fact you are doing."*

- I Thessalonians 5:14: *"And we urge you, brothers, warn those who are idle, encourage the timid, help the weak, be patient with everyone."*

- 2 Thessalonians 2:17: *"Encourage your hearts and strengthen yourself in every good deed and word."*

> **The encourager helps someone apply the command given in Philippians 4:8**
>
> ***"Whatever is true, whatever is noble, whatever is right, whatever is pure, whatever is lovely, whatever is admirable—if anything is excellent or praiseworthy— think about such things."***

- Titus 2:6: *"Similarly, encourage the young men to be self-controlled."*

- Titus 2:15: *"These, then, are the things you should teach. Encourage and rebuke with all authority."*

- Hebrews 3:13: *"But encourage one another daily, as long as it is called Today, so that none of you may be hardened by sin's deceitfulness."*

- Hebrews 10:25: *"Let us not give up meeting together, as some are in the habit of doing, but let us encourage one another—and all the more as you see the Day approaching."*

So, what does an encourager do? The most valuable thing that an encourager does is to help someone apply the command given in Philippians 4:8, *"Finally, brethren, whatsoever things are true, whatsoever things are honest, whatsoever things are just, whatsoever things are pure, whatsoever things are lovely, whatsoever things are of good report; if there be any virtue, and if there be any praise, think on these things."*

This is what I did with Samira. While I played several roles my most important role was to be an encourager and a point of accountability. I was extra careful not to teach or advise because I could not fully relate to her life circumstances. The best thing that I did was to remind her that I believed in her and that she was not doing this study by herself, but with Jesus at her side.

God worked in Samira's life directing her in a very interesting way. Most of her years were spent in financial management, but Samira's StrengthsFinder profile included **empathy, restorative, positivity, responsibility, and relator**. In the following years, God gave her unique opportunities to care for and provide support to several aging people in Canada. By many measurements, she had finally found her sweet spot.

I know you may be too busy to engage in a long course on encouragement. Should you have some time, watch these video clips:

- https://www.youtube.com/watch?v=sMxVTzWndlc
- https://www.youtube.com/watch?v=zDgwtVvB7Dg
- https://www.youtube.com/watch?v=LYICprx_YDs
- https://maxlucado.com/watch/encourage-one-another-100-happy-people-pt-2/

When you are done with that, take time and look for some short articles on encouragement or how to become an encourager. Remember, this is an important skill that will serve you in all aspects of your life.

Application: What Can You Do?

Examining the ministry development framework, do you know anyone who needs encouragement? Do you know anyone who:

- Has lost, or is at risk of losing his or her job?

- Is struggling with self-worth or self-esteem?

- Is discouraged with his or her work-life?

- Doesn't see hope or purpose in what he or she does from day today?

Picture yourself with someone who fits any of the above needs. How can you modify my experience with Samira and adapt it to your world so you can also help others in your world? Ask God to give bring to your mind a specific person. For ease of description let us call this person, Jane.   For an exercise try to answer the following questions:

- **About you: What Strengths and Motivation:**
    - o What natural talents? Use adjectives to describe them.
    - o What Knowledge + Skill + Experience will help you relate to Jane?
    - o What are your motivations? Why would you wish to help Jane?

- **About your Jane:** What Strengths (Talents X Knowledge + Skills + Experience) has she been given? What are her needs or life challenges?

- **About tools and processes:** I would like you to think of:
    - o **Connecting tools and processes.** What can you do to connect with people like Jane? How can you use

> the "How are You card" or the Wellness Gauge as effective tools?

- o **Serving tools and processes:** How can you best use the Strengths Self Study tools? Remember these are tools to be adapted to your style and need.

How does it work in real life? If the person expresses interest, all you have to do is sent the link to the Strengths Self-Study resources and start playing your role as an encourager. We live in very fortunate times. The internet has expanded our reach. You and I can help people in faraway places as well as neighbors next door. Over the years we have given the Strengths Workshop to people as old as an 84-year-old woman in Honduras and a 16-year-old high school student in Toronto. The Strengths Self-Study is designed to fulfill the same objective so you can use it far and wide.

- **About Jesus:** Remember, there is never a perfect fit. Jesus will fill in the gaps. He is more than able. How would you like to ask Him to help you so you can help your Jane?

With this simple tool, you have the potential of impacting the majority of people around the world. How do I know? Based on research by Gallup *"People who use their strengths every day are three times more likely to report having an excellent quality of life, six times more likely to be engaged at work, 8% more productive and 15% less likely to quit their jobs." Regretfully **only** 17% use their Strengths every day."*

Application: What is Your Role?

Many of us feel very inadequate when separated by many miles. I often fear the risk of misunderstanding or miscommunicating. This inadequacy can be reduced when I know that Jesus is our partner in this process. Despite the miles that separate us He is there bridging the gap and even if there are misunderstandings, He can bring his perfect knowledge.

Over about a 3-month relationship with Samira, I played several roles. But the primary one was that of an encourager. My relationship started as a listener. I asked a lot of questions. She talked and I listened. In the process, I played the role of a Resource directing her to websites and places where she could learn about her Strengths. Later in a small way, I played the role of an advisor when she asked me specific questions about a few matters where I had knowledge or experience.

Many times during our conversations I felt stuck and helpless or in over my head. This is the time when I would often stop and ask the Lord, "Father, what role do you want me to play now?" This happened when Samira shared that she feared being locked up at home with her husband who has been unemployed for 28 years and has developed a very depressing and negative attitude towards everything in life. She asked for advice I could not give. That was the moment when the Lord said, "Just pray and leave it to Me. Stop everything and just pray with her."

With the Holy Spirit as your partner, consider the following situation. If you were in a similar place with your friend, Jane, what roles would you be likely to play? How would you define your roles? Using the roles diagram as your guide in defining the role of "Encourager":

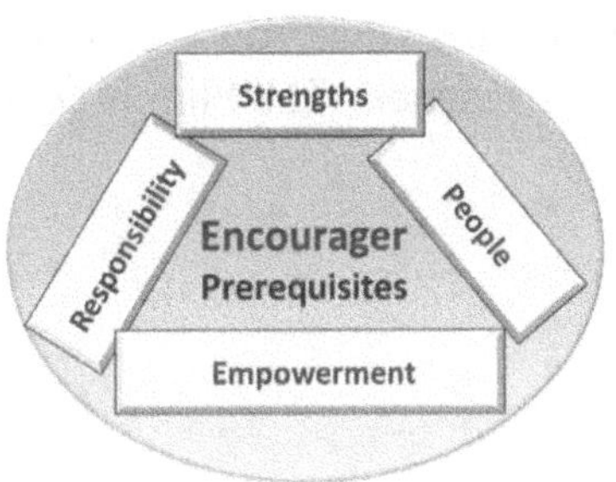

- **Encourager Prerequisites:** What are the prerequisite qualifications for this role?
- **Strengths:** What Strengths do you bring?
  - o   Natural Talents? Use adjectives to describe them.

- o Knowledge + skills + experience? List the most likely to relate to Jane.

- **Who are the people** in your role?

  - o Who are the partners who will support you?

  - o Who are the teachable people or clients other than Jane who need your help? What are their strengths and needs?

- **What responsibilities** do you have? What are you accountable for?

- **What empowerment** do you need? Be sure to consider tools and resources as well as how much time you are prepared to invest or spend with Jane.

Tell Jesus

- Go back and examine the thoughts shared in this section.

- Journal and summarize your observations. Write them down.

Share what you learned as a written conversation with Jesus. Remember, He is listening; He said I am with you always.

Tell Jesus what you would like to do as a result of what you have learned. Tell Him how you want Him to help you.

STRENGTHS VIDEO WORKSHOP

Playing the Role of Organizer

Pedro was born to be a leader. From his early childhood, he was the kid that brought other kids together, organized football games and parties, started fights, and put out some. As he got into his teen years his Dad could see the risks awaiting his son. Drug gangs were on the hunt for kids with natural leadership talents.

"Pedro, you are a good fighter, you should be in the military using real guns, not toy tankers." This was the image instilled in young Pedro's mind. His military career took hold of all his imagination. He could not wait until he turned 17 to enlist. In the military school, he applied competitive and controlling natural talents that were in him before he was even born. By age 21 he had graduated from the military college and held the rank of Lieutenant.

With a big grin on his face, he told me, *"I told myself, I am going to marry the prettiest and wealthiest girl in town, and I did. By 28 I had a large house and 3 kids."* Regretfully at home, Pedro used the same talents and tried to play the same role he played in the military. On his 30th birthday, his wife handed him the divorce papers and taking full custody of the children she moved into her parent's estate with them.

As it often happens, released from the role of father and husband Pedro gave all his passion to the application of his talents in his military career. A few weeks after his 44th birthday, he was eligible for retirement and a very comfortable pension with lots of benefits. *"Now, I can take life easy and have more fun,"* he thought to himself.

After a few weeks and months of fun and idle living, his life became empty and hopeless. His kids who were estranged from him for such a long time refused to spend time with him. He thought of reenlisting in the military, but his pride would not let him. He recalls, *"I ran out of gas; I could not even get out of bed in the morning."*

In his desperation, he thought maybe he should get married again. That led him to church. Instead of finding a wife, Pedro found Jesus waiting for him. His leadership talents and his "can do" attitude attracted the pastor. Pedro applied the same Strengths He applied in his military life and became engaged in all aspects of church life.

It was Pedro, who picked us up in his flashy big truck as we arrived at the airport in Panama, Central America. As he drove us around from one event to another, I was impressed by his organizational talents. One morning, Pedro picked me up for breakfast. He said, *"I am going to take you out to a very special place because I have something special to discuss."* After ordering our food, I asked, *"What is on your mind?"* He leaned over as if he wanted to tell me a military secret. *"In the Strengths workshop, you challenged me to think of the fact that in the eyes of my Heavenly Father I am still a little child. You asked me what I want to be when I grow up. I have been thinking about this. When I grow up, I want to be like you."* His words brought tears into my eyes. I was honored and humbled by his desire.

Pedro had played a major part in organizing our workshops and the one on one coaching meetings we had in Panama. Out of that, he envisioned how *"he could be like me."* He developed a vision of doing leadership training seminars and workshops using our material. He had healthy relationships with friends, church contacts as well as business leaders and ex-military colleagues.

This is exactly what he did. It started with a small group of friends gathered in his church hall. He followed the same structure we did in our workshops using the Spanish Strengths Video Workshop. Over time he invested time and learned more about Strengths and their application to many aspects of life and professions. From there he developed a new set of management and leadership tools that combined and modified our Strengths Workshop resources with other tools and concepts from his military leadership training.

What Do Organizers Do?

Over the past years, we offered the Living Your Strengths Workshop in a half-day of about 4.5 hours. The format of the workshop was simple:

- Participants had to do personal homework, about 2-3 hours.

- The 4.5 hours were divided into 8-10 presentation segments.

- Each segment included short teaching followed by an exercise done in groups or pairs with very little intervention of the part of the teacher.

The Strengths Video workshop offers content that is very similar to the Living Your Strengths Workshop. The format is almost identical. And the allocated time is about the same. The only key difference is replacing the live teacher with a video clip. Each teaching video clip offers very detailed instructions regarding the discussion exercises.

With the simplicity of the technology, the role of the facilitator becomes more of a host and organizer. This simple process keeps the administrative overhead to a minimum. The needed promotion, homework, and delivery tools are all available. This will enable anyone to deliver the workshop regardless of group size. You can deliver it to a group of 4 people in a living room or an auditorium filled with 500 people.

Think back of Pedro, what do you think made him successful?

- He had a passion for helping people.

- He was teachable.

- He was committed.

- He did not have to invest a lot of time developing any tools or resources.

- He started small by using the Strengths Video Workshop to impact people he cared for and who trusted him.

Application: What Can You do?

The Strengths resources are provided as tools in the process of making disciples and of building relationships for the Kingdom of God. Just like Pedro, you and I have a far greater influence than we realize. Regretfully, we seldom connect with these good people because we do not have an appropriate framework for developing our relationships.

There are people in your neighborhoods, work environments, or even family circles who need you. These people would welcome your desire to connect with them and show them you care. Start small. Picture yourself like Pedro with a small group of people in your living room or church hall.

For an exercise try to answer the following questions:

- **About you: What Strengths and Motivation?**
    - What natural talents? Use adjectives to describe them.
    - What Knowledge + Skill + Experience do you bring to this group?
    - What are your motivations? Why would do you wish to help?
- **About your group:** What Strengths (Talents X Knowledge + Skills + Experience) have they been given? What are their needs or life challenges?
- **About tools and processes:** I would like you to think of:
    - **Connecting tools and processes.** What can you do to connect with your people? How can you use the "How are You Card" or the Wellness Gauge as effective connection tools?

Serving tools and processes: How can you best use the Strengths Video Workshop? Remember these are tools to be adapted to your style and need. Regarding playing your role we will provide some guidance on how to do that.

- **About Jesus:** Remember, there is never a perfect fit. Jesus will fill in the gaps. He is more than able. How would you like to ask Him to help you so you can help your Jane?

Remember you can have a great impact on the lives of many. Based on research by Gallup "People who use their strengths every day are three times more likely to report having an excellent quality of life, six times more likely to be engaged at work, 8% more productive and 15% less likely to quit their jobs." Regretfully, **only** 17% use their Strengths every day. You can play a major part in helping people discover and use their Strengths.

More About Delivery Process

Promotions:

You have our permission to download, edit, and print any of the promotion tools available on the resource page. However, the best promotional tool is a personal invitation. Starting with the "How are You card" as a connection tool, make it a habit to engage with people. Where appropriate, ask you partners to help you with your promotion. For those who are interested, collect their contact information and send them links to the appropriate web pages. Follow up two days later to answer any questions. Be sure to explain the need for commitment.

General Logistics

- **Group Size:**
  - o The number of participants is limited only by the available space and technology for the video presentation. You need to be sure that all members:
    - Can see the TV or projected video
    - Can easily partner to discuss the exercises with minimal distractions

- **Location:** With the help of your host, choose a home, church, or office that is easy to find and can accommodate the needed equipment and easy seating for discussion without a lot of distractions. Let your host decide what kind of refreshments would be least disruptive to the group activity, keeping in mind the limited time allowed.

- **Equipment and Supplies**: Long before you start, be sure to:
  - o Download the video clips and back them up on a DVD or memory stick.
  - o Test your video or projection equipment.

Registration

- Confirm the correct name, phone, and e-mail.

- Edit and e-mail the following registration confirmation to each person.

Subject: Confirmation, The Strengths Workshop

Dear (First Name),

I am very pleased that you will be joining us in the Strengths Workshop. I will be praying for you as you seek to discover your Strengths and apply them to fulfill your life callings. In preparation, please:

1. Remember that we will meet:

    o **Location:** Your Church, 22 Lover Road, Heaven Town

    o **Date:** Saturday February 12, 202X XX/Month/ Year

    o **Time:** 8:30 AM – 1:00PM

2. Download the mandatory homework which you will find at https://nomoreoverload.com/Data-Web/Notes/SF2.0-Alt.pdf. Please read this VERY carefully and follow the provided step by step instructions. Please note that this workshop is designed to be participatory. Your good preparation will not only impact how much you will get from the workshop but also how you can collaborate with others in the discussion. **Please give this your top priority.**

If you have any questions, please feel free to call me at (phone #).

Sincerely,

Signed

Personal Preparation:

As the Lord leads you, two or three days before your workshop:

- Pray for yourself and each of your members.

- Review the videos and do the related exercises.

- Write any notes that God may bring to your mind in preparation.

- Go over the timelines. Imagine and define your timeline expectations.

Facilitation Process

Two or three days before the workshop phone your participants.

- o Answer any questions they may have about needed preparation.

- o Encourage them to pray for themselves and

- o Encourage them to arrive on time.

As your participants arrive your role is primarily that of a good host who ensures the smooth flow of the timelines. The participant notes and the videos provide detailed step by step instructions of what will happen during the workshop.

The end of each video includes specific instructions for an exercise break. Use your discretion about how much time you provide for each break. We feel 10 to 15 minutes should be adequate.

Often people say, *"I wish we had more discussion time."* The first and last video will address this point by recommending the participants take advantage of the **Strengths Learning Lab** which we hope you may consider offering as a follow-up. The evaluation sheet, which is the last page in the participants' notes, is the tool for you to follow up with those interested in the Strengths Learning Lab.

Application: What is Your Role?

Most of my 35 years in the corporate world were spent in organizational change management. During that time, I learned that administrative overhead and complexity are the greatest enemies of progress and change. While it is important to do things well, the cost of perfection can be very high. So, we encourage you to keep it simple.

With the Holy Spirit as your partner use the roles diagram as your guide in defining the role of "organizer":

Strengths

Responsibility

People

Organizer
Prerequisites

Empowerment

72

- **Organizer Prerequisites:** What are the role prerequisite qualifications?

- **Strengths:** What Strengths do you bring?
  - o Natural Talents? Use adjectives to describe them.
  - o Knowledge + skills + experience? List what you may apply.

- **Who are the people** in your role?
  - o Who are the partners who will support you?
  - o Who are the teachable people or clients that you hope will come to your workshop? What are their Strengths and needs?

- **What responsibilities** do you have? What are you accountable for?

- **What empowerment** do you need? Be sure to consider tools and resources as well as how much time you are prepared to invest or spend in doing this ministry.

Tell Jesus

- Go back and examine the thoughts shared in this section.

- Journal and summarize your observations. Write them down.

Share what you learned as a written conversation with Jesus. Remember, He is listening and He said I am with you always.

STRENGTHS LEARNING LAB

Playing the Role of Facilitator

The Jews in the days of Jesus had one great thing going for them. They knew the Scripture. However, they were at a great disadvantage because they misinterpreted it. In His teaching, Jesus leveraged that knowledge and challenged them in the application of what they knew.

Later we see Paul following a similar model in his teaching. He leveraged the background and knowledge inherent in his listeners. From there he challenged them to think differently and make personal application and commitment.

It is a well-established fact that when individuals take more ownership of their learning, they are more committed to the application of what they learn. For this reason, we will approach your leadership role in the Strengths Learning Lab to be that of a facilitator of a learning process, not a teacher or advisor.

What Do Facilitators Do?

If we examine dictionaries for insight, we find terms like *"a facilitator as someone who assists the progress of."*

Facilitation is a relationship between one person, "a facilitator," and a group of people who have a common

In effective facilitation, the client defines the objective BUT the facilitator controls the process and the tools.

purpose and may have different Strengths and/or needs. The facilitator has **no personal interest** in the outcome except the common good of the group and the objectives of its participants.

The role of the facilitator can be quite diverse **BUT** seldom based on his knowledge. At its heart, the success of the facilitator is based on his or her ability to engage the group members in achieving the group's purpose and objectives.   Good facilitators have three critical qualities:

1. They listen well.
2. They ask good questions, and
3. They apply the right tools and processes.

First Example:

We learned of issues and conflict arising between two of our friends who were key leaders at their church. We had prayed for them and shared our concerns with each of them. Now we felt the Lord nudging us to do something more.   We sensed that the Lord was calling us to play the role of a facilitator.   So, we asked each of them if they trusted us enough to facilitate a meeting to resolve some of the conflicts between them.   To our delight, they agreed and we set a time to meet in our home.

"Now, Lord, how do I play the role of the facilitator?" The Lord said, *"Pray."* Then the Lord reminded me of what my mother once told me, *"If you get stuck between the onion and the onion skin you get nothing but the stink."* This has been a key principle in my facilitation and coaching practice for many years. My wife and I prayed for wisdom.

As my wife and I prayed, we believed God wanted us to apply a very simple process but a very powerful tool. As homework, I sent our two friends an e-mail asking them to study Matthew 18:15-17 *"If your brother sins against you, go and show him his fault, just between the two of you. If he listens to you, you have won your brother over. But if he will not listen, take one or two others along, so that 'every matter may be established by the testimony of two or three witnesses.' If he refuses to listen to them, tell it to the church; and if he refuses to listen even to the church, treat him as you would a pagan or a tax collector."* I told them that we will use this passage when we meet.

When our friends arrived, my wife pointed them to the dining table where she had set a fresh pot of coffee and some cookies and fruit. We gave them two Bibles and asked them to turn to the same passage in Matthew 18:15-17.

After reading this passage, I told them that we believe in them. We all agreed that the objective is to fulfill the steps of the reconciliation process outlined in this passage. We know that God wants to help them apply it. They agreed not to leave the room until they, with the Lord's help, had fully applied the first step in this process. They also agreed that they understood the implication of the second and third step which would have to be applied if the first step did not fulfill the desired reconciliation.

My wife and I left them and went to our bedroom to pray for them. About an hour later they called us to thank us for the facilitation role we played. They reported that by the grace of God they had made very good progress. As we prayed together it was a delight to see them hug each other with tears of joy.

Second Example

Returning from our holiday there was a voice mail message. Thomas, the chair of our elders' board, was asking me to take part in a very important meeting next Saturday. The meeting involved himself, the pastor, and two other high-profile congregants.   The background for this request was that during *the* last congregational meeting, **which we did not attend, thankfully**, some disagreements led to hurting words and unkind behavior.

> *In his best-selling book, Just Listen, author, Dr. Mark Goulston, writes,*
>
> **"People do not change because of what you say, rather, much more because of what you get them to say."**

My wife and I were relative newcomers to that church. I wondered why he would ask me to attend, especially when I was not at the meeting and had no knowledge of what took place. Before accepting, I asked Thomas why he chose me for such an honor. He said, "We *feel that since you were not at the meeting you are likely to be more objective.*"

Being careful that I would not get dragged into unrealistic expectations of what I could accomplish, I asked, *"What role do you expect me to play?"* After some discussion, we agreed that I would act as a facilitator. I agreed, provided that all the others wanted me to play that role so I asked for permission to connect with the other men by phone.

Before calling these men, I prayed Lord, help me clarify my role. I felt the Lord asking me to just listen to their hearts and feelings. With each of these men, I started the conversation by thanking him for trusting me to facilitate the coming session. This was followed by questions like:

- Can you please tell me what happened?

- How did that make you feel?

- What offended you the most?

- What would you have done differently?

- What do you think can be done to bring about reconciliation?

Then I asked if he would write down exactly what he told me on a separate piece of paper and bring it to the meeting. I expressed that this is mandatory homework.

As a facilitator, I followed a simple facilitation model based on the acronym, **GROW**, and a very common coaching process as well. This is how the meeting went:

- After praying, I started the meeting asking each person to confirm that the **G**oal is to bring reconciliation to the conflict and hurt that followed the congregational meeting. They all agreed.

- Following that, I gave everyone 10 uninterrupted minutes to read exactly what he has written in his homework and share what he believed was the **R**eal issue that led to the conflict. I took notes. I summarized what each person shared to make sure I understand their thoughts and feelings.

- Then I asked one of them to be the scribe on a whiteboard as we listed the **O**ptions that could lead to reconciliation.

Prayerfully, we narrowed the option to the one that is most biblically-based.

- To **W**rap up the meeting, I asked each one to describe the next step that he was prepared to take as a follow-up.

- Then the pastor closed with prayer.

Third Example:

Shortly after we were married, we joined a Navigators Bible study group.   The "Nav's" as they are called is a Bible study ministry that started in the US Navy but it is the best known for its work among students on university campuses around the world. The years of our involvement with the Nav's have been a great contributor to our growth both spiritually and emotionally.

Another ministry that has had an impact on our lives is Bible Study Fellowship (**BSF**). For more than 24 years my wife has been a member or a leader with *BSF*.   Almost half a million people in more than 120 countries around the world are impacted by the ministry of *BSF* every week. The leadership development training that my wife has had through *BSF* has impacted her role in the church, our community, and even her roles in our home.

You may wonder, apart from the Bible and the Holy Spirit, what contributes to the success of such great Bible study ministries. Certainly, it is not money or a large organization. For example, apart from a very small headquarters staff that focuses on content development and logistics, *BSF* is a volunteer-run organization. **The secret lies in:**

1. **Self-motivated participants.**   Group members are expected to invest in their study using pre-distributed study tools and predefined questions.   They are also expected to share what the Lord has taught them with others in the group weekly meeting.

2. **Self-study toolset:** Members receive predefined personal study notes that lead to application-oriented questions. They are expected to commit to doing the personal study before coming to the group meeting.

3. **Committed leaders or facilitators:** Leaders are trained to listen well. BSF training asks facilitators to limit the time they talk to less than 20% of the time.   This allows the participants 80- 90% of the time to share what they have learned from their study. Also, group meetings are a platform in developing personal one on one follow up discipleship conversations.

4. **Transferable low overhead process**: The principle of having transferable training tools is used by many successful organizations. Regretfully, as programs grow, they gain complexity and administrative overhead. **Here we must highlight that there is power in simplicity.** Having well-defined roles that are simply communicated is critical. This simplicity has allowed organizations like BSF to flourish even in the poorest parts of the world.

Fourth Example

Our son Noel teaches at one of the largest American universities. This is his first full-time university teaching career. Interested in his wellbeing we asked how he is doing. He told us that he loves his teaching roles. He shared that one of the greatest contributors to his success and enjoyment is using **"the flipped classroom model."** Noel explained that this model is growing in popularity especially among younger educators.   To help us understand this model, Noel explained it is similar to the Bible study discipleship format used by his youth pastor years ago. For your interest see YouTube at https://youtu.be/qdKzSq_t8k8

Asking the Right Question

Good journalism is founded on the integrity of reporting. Journalists are told that if you do not ask the right questions do not expect a good answer. Good questions have a purpose, lead to objectives, define goals, and/or accomplish progress towards good results. Good facilitators spend a lot of time thinking and planning their good questions. Questions are more powerful than answers. There are many types of questions. For our purpose, I would like to highlight only three and provide you with some examples for each.

Revealing questions encourage creativity and imagination. They invite different thinking. Revealing questions challenge limitations, beliefs, and established priorities.

o   Where are you right now concerning …?
o   What do you like about where you are now…?
o   What don't you like about where you are now…?
o   What do you care about most deeply regarding…?
o   What are your unique strengths, skills, experiences…?
o   How did you feel about...?
o   What other pictures can you see when you think of...?
o   What values do you hold most dear...?
o   Who else can you consider for...?

Ownership questions encourage taking responsibility or define **"SMART"** goals and action steps.

o   What part are you playing in...?
o   What have you done that contributed to...?
o   What could you have done differently…?
o   What do you want to do about...?
o   How can you change...?

Direct questions seek focus, action, and/or accountability. When used wisely, these questions can help ensure that the conversation provides the greatest benefit.

o   What progress did you make regarding...?
o   How will you communicate...?
o   What are you prepared to do next...?

- o When do you plan to...?
- o How can we be sure that you will...?
- o How can you share the change you are making to help others facing similar challenges?

Application: What Can You Do?

There are some important facts that you must remember before you start:

1. The objectives of the Strengths Learning Lab are well defined and cannot be changed. They are to help people:

    a. Discover their God-given Strengths as a reflection of God's image.

    b. Develop a process to define their God-given roles and fulfill their life callings.

2. The primary teaching tools are well established and should not be changed. They are the Strengths web-based, self-study toolset.

3. The pre-study homework is mandatory and cannot be replaced.

Please go back and examine the description of the ministry framework we provided earlier. Picture yourself in a small Bible study group with some very keen disciples. How can you apply this framework so you can fulfill your role as a facilitator?

For an exercise try to answer the following questions:

- **About you:**

- o **Strengths?** What Strengths has God given you that will help facilitate and serve this group? (Talents X Knowledge + Skill + Experience)

- o **What is your motivation?** Why would do you wish to help people?

- **About Your Group:**

  - o **Strengths?** What Strengths do you see in them?

  - o **Needs:** What common needs and life challenges are they likely to have?

- **About tools and processes:** I would like you to think of:

  - o **Connecting tools and processes.** What can you do to connect and engage with potential group members? While advertising and promotion tools may be helpful, the greatest model was given to us by Jesus using personal invitation.

  - o **Serving tools and processes:** How can you best use the tools provided? You will find online all the tools you are likely to need. While we will provide you with a very descriptive well-proven process and action plan, we want you to have the freedom to follow the guidance of the Holy Spirit.

- **About Jesus:** Remember, there is never a perfect fit. DO NOT AIM FOR PERFECTION. Jesus will fill in the gaps. He is more than able. Ask him to help you so you can help your people.

Application: What Is Your Role?

Jesus said I am with you always. With this in view, I am learning that even in the simplest encounters I can seek His input. How do I do this? I simply take a moment and ask, "Lord, what is my role here?"

Facilitator Prerequisites

Important facts to remember:

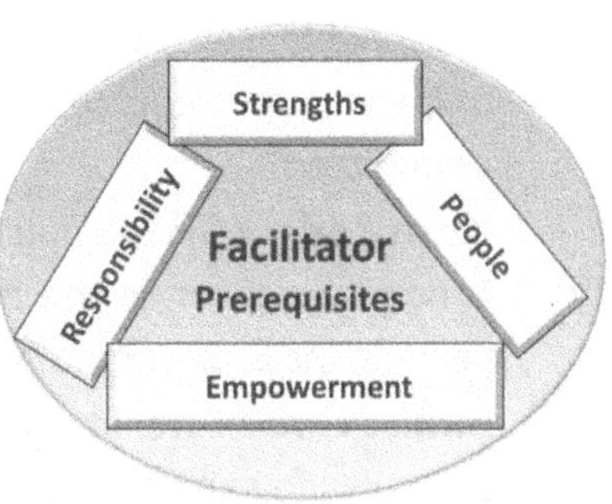

The Strengths Learning Lab (**SLL**) is a relational and discipleship ministry. The role of **SF** is a great opportunity to help you grow in knowing yourself and others but most importantly of knowing Jesus Christ himself. Jesus calls you to be his co-laborer not so much because He needs you, rather because He can enjoy your fellowship and desires to help you become more like Himself.

Remember, *"You can never lead people to where you are not going."* For this reason, you must:

- Be committed to spending time with Jesus and *"being with Jesus to learn from Jesus to become like Jesus."*
- Seek to grow as a student of Strengths.
- Invest time learning about the application of Strengths in your own life.
- "Practice." Professional facilitators call their work a *"practice."* This is your God-given opportunity to practice and grow as a child of God.
- **Stay teachable.** Allow the Holy Spirit to use others to lead you and support you. As often as you can, seek the input and advice of others.
- Seek the evaluation and candid input of your group
- Prioritize the time you spend with your overseer. His primary role is to shepherd and care for you.

Strengths

Using the Strengths formula let us attempt to shed some light on the impact of Strengths on your leadership development:

- **Talents:** One of the best ways to describe talents is by using adjectives. Some adjectives that may describe a good **SF** are personable, relational, empathetic, organized, communicative, understanding, curious, teachable, open-minded, and committed.
- **Knowledge:** The required knowledge is minimum and the **SF** is not a teacher. In the flipped classroom model, each participant is expected to do his or her self-study.
- **Skills:** Good listening and the ability to ask questions are primary life skills for most of us.   These skills do not come naturally, but most often can be developed by persistent practice, self-observation, and coaching.
- **Experience:** Supported by your overseer and understanding participants you will gain experience upon experience provided you reflect:
  - Enthusiasm for the possibility of being a co-laborer with Christ.
  - Commitment to invest the time to be disciplined and disciple others.
  - A sincere desire to apply Matthew 25 and bring great returns for the Kingdom of God.
  - A teachable heart that accepts the authority of the church leadership structure and suggestions for ongoing improvement from the ministry overseer, group participants, and others.

People

Your role is all about relationships. This is a great opportunity for your life to be impacted by people and for you to impact the lives of other people.   We will discuss two types of people.

Important People

If you plan to do something significant for Christ, it is only natural to expect that the devil will seek to obstruct you or even destroy you. Ministry is a dangerous place for those who want to do it alone.   Ecclesiastes 4:12 highlights the importance of relationships in ministry.   *"By yourself, you're unprotected. With a friend, you can face the worst. Can you round up a third? A three-stranded rope isn't easily snapped."* The Message.   In addition to the Lord Jesus, by your side, there are at least two partners that support the role of **SF.** They are:

- **Substitute Facilitator:** The substitute facilitator plays a supporting and partnership role. Being equipped with different strengths, ministry tasks can be assigned differently. Developing one on one relationships could also be enhanced by having different talents and relationship building skills. Take time to invest in developing this relationship.
- **Overseer / Shepard:** The **SF** is accountable to the Strengths Ministry Overseer who plays shepherding and development roles. You must prioritize this relationship. Your overseer is expected to pray for you weekly and meet with you at least once a month for support and accountability. Make that your priority as well.

About the Overseer

Let us talk more about the role of the overseer. The overseer is entrusted with an awesome privilege and responsibility. While some may think that the primary responsibility is finding the right facilitators, shepherding, and developing those God instructs into His care is far greater and more critical.

Jesus highlights the most important role of the overseer in His conversation with Peter in John 15:15-17 *"When they had finished eating, Jesus said to Simon Peter, 'Simon son of John, do you truly love me more than these?' 'Yes, Lord,' he said, 'you know that I love you.' Jesus said, 'Feed my lambs.' Again, Jesus said, 'Simon son of John, do you truly love me?' He answered, 'Yes, Lord, you know that I love you.' Jesus said, 'Take care of my sheep.' The third time he said to him,*

'Simon son of John, do you love me?' Peter was hurt because Jesus asked him the third time, 'Do you love me? He said, 'Lord, you know all things; you know that I love you.' Jesus said, 'Feed my sheep.''' While recruiting and administration may be important, the primary responsibilities of the overseer are shepherding and developing the **SF.**

If you are called to be an overseer here is what may be considered a basic action plan or responsibility:

- **Pray.** Pray for each *SF* by name weekly.   As you pray ask the Lord to reveal to you what you should do for His precious sheep.
- **Connect:** Once a week, reach out to your team of *SFs* by phone, mail, or text. Be an encourager.
- **Meet:** At least once a month meet with each SF to assess how he or she is doing physically, emotionally, spiritually, and relating to work-life issues. You may wish to use the How are You card and the Wellness Gauge as tools.
- **Observe:** Attend at least one session per term to observe the *SF* in action so you can offer:
    - **Encouragement:** Ask God to show you some positive attributes, observations, or results that you can share with the **SF.**
    - **Corrections:** Seek ways to help the *SF* develop his or her skills.
- **Evaluate:** Meet with the *SF* and others to evaluate the effectiveness of this ministry.
- **Report:** Communicate as expected by the church leadership as the God-given authority over your role.

Teachable people

The purpose is to draw people into a closer relationship with Jesus. The teachable people are the clients or beneficiaries of your facilitation and discipleship process. There are three ways teachable people will be introduced to the *SLL:*

- **Promotion and advertising:** These are the traditional and least effective ways.
- **The Living Your Strengths Workshop:** For those who are unable to make the 12-week *SLL* commitment this 4.5-hour outreach-oriented session is a good stepping stone.
- **Personal Invitation:** This is by far the most effective way. Following the model of Jesus, we see that He invited others to join him. Prompted by the Holy Spirit, you, your team, and others who have taken the *SLL* should be encouraged to invite others on the journey. This invitation process should include all those interested in helping people on the discipleship pathway.

Responsibilities

Shepherd

The *SLL* is a relationship-building and discipleship ministry. This is your opportunity to build one on one relationship for greater impact. You are a shepherd of those God will entrust into this unique relationship. This involves effort, time, and sensitivity to the Holy Spirit. In John 10:14 Jesus provides a picture that best describes the role of a shepherd. He is the good shepherd and He is calling you to partner with Him. Here are some tips to help you:

- Commit to praying for each person at least once a week. Pray that:
  - God would transform their lives according to His perfect will.
  - God would increase your love and concern for each person as you pray by name.
  - The Holy Spirit gives you the understanding and wisdom you need to love them.
  - The Holy Spirit enables members to remain committed to studying and applying what they learn.

- Make that commitment known to your group members. See every person as a unique child of God. Getting to uncover their hidden gems is an adventure you can take with Jesus as your guide.

- Offer to connect with each person weekly using the most appropriate tool (phone, email, texting…).

- Seek opportunities for one on one connection. This will help you get to know individuals as the Lord leads you. This is an honest desire for friendship, not a task for a checklist.

Facilitation

This is the time when your preparation and dependence on the Lord are engaged for a great impact on your group. Remember you are not a teacher. **Avoid the temptation to teach and or give long explanations.** The success of your group meeting does not depend on what you say but much more on what your group members will share about what God has already revealed to them through their homework. We are not asking you to share your opinion or ask new questions. Rather you must make sure that the **TOP** priority is given to your team members in sharing what they have uncovered in their self-study. If you do not make this a VERY clear priority, it will diminish the value of the self-study part and your team members will stop doing their homework.

Here are some general tips that may help you:

- Avoid dead time. Have a simple ice breaker or kind words **in case you need them.**

- **Remember,** your body language and eye contact are your most effective communication tool. Your body language impacts as much as **60% of your communication skills.** Practice this and it will serve you well in all aspects of your life.

- Be engaged. Listen well:
  - Practice effective active listening.

- o Pay attention to the correct body language.
- o **Smile. Smiles are contagious**. Show that you are enjoying this discussion.

- Encourage transparency and integrity by being a model of honesty.

- Lead by providing a safe environment. Make sure that everyone can participate without fearing others' responses.

- Always highlight the priority of the self-study homework.

- Make sure no one is left out. Involve all members in the discussion.

- Avoid dead time by asking good questions.

- You are not an advisor. Avoid giving advice. It is best to rephrase your opinion into a question that stimulates thinking and answers by the group.

About Your First Meeting

Your first meeting is critical. The first impression of your shepherding and leadership skills is set in this first meeting. Through this meeting, you set the expectations that will last for the rest of the time you are together. **Here are some tips that may help you:**

- Before your group arrives be VERY organized. Have your room well set up to create the expected atmosphere.

- Take time to pray by yourself or with your host and substitute facilitator.

- In this session, you can plan to speak about 50% of the time.

- Be very WARM and hospitable.

- Your body language and eye contact are the most effective communication tools.

- Welcome and engage with each person as he or she arrives.

- Provide a copy of the member information and member agreement for each person.

- Avoid dead time. Have a simple icebreaker on hand.

- Your first session is a good time to get acquainted. You may like to start with some icebreakers.

- Set an example. Share the impact Strengths has had on your life.

- Share your contact info, top Strengths, and what you wish to get out of this workshop.

- Have every group member share the same information.

- This is the time to correct the member information as needed.

  o Since each group member is unique, you may wish to keep a separate sheet of paper for each person where you record important thoughts, needs, and/or prayer requests for each person. Update it after each group meeting. This is a helpful tool for your weekly contact and one on one coaching conversations.

- Review the member agreement and set clear expectations. Have each member sign his or her copy.

- Give those who wish to drop out the option to do so gracefully.

- Close in prayer.

- Evaluate this session with your substitute facilitator.

About Your Weekly Meeting

All your participants are entrusting you with their valuable time. In an average group meeting, you are a steward of more than 8 to 12 hours of people's time. Invest that time wisely. Have a plan. Here is a suggested outline:

> **Note: While you are encouraged to follow the above pattern, have the freedom to inject some variation to create interest for yourself and your team.**

1. Be sure to do your lessons. Do not rely on old memory or experience.

2. Engage with people as they arrive. Welcome each by name. Make them comfortable. Be very WARM and hospitable.

3. Start on time with a short one-minute prayer.

4. Follow the homework questions as the priority for your discussions. This is critical for if you do not, your people will stop doing the homework.

5. To highlight the priority of doing homework, use open questions like:

    o "Joe, what stands out to you as a result of what you studied?"

    o "Sally, how do you see God working in your life based on your study?"

    o "Tom, where do you see an application of…"

6. Be sure not to miss anyone from this part of the discussion.

7. Follow up by asking about questions, issues, or concerns that may arise from the personal study:

    o Communicate interest and avoid the temptation to jump in with a quick answer.

    o Encourage others to provide an answer or input instead of you.

    o If you have an opinion, instead of providing it, phrase it into a question. **This is a powerful facilitation and coaching tool that needs a lot of practice.** The purpose is to help your group find answers to their challenges.

8. Follow the same pattern by asking the application questions:

    o "Sally, what is the most important thing you learned this week?"

> *The primary function of the facilitator is to understand. Not to solve, heal, make better, or be wise…The magic is that it is in that moment of understanding, the clients understand for themselves, become more aware, and are then in a position to make better decisions and choices than they would have done…*
>
> *This is how facilitation is profoundly simple and simply profound.*
>
> *Myles Downey, adapted from Effective Coaching*

     o "What do you plan to do about that?"

9. Prepare other open-ended questions should you need them.

10. Plan for some backup exercises from the Strengths Workshop Book. These can be used if you have more time with the group.

11. If you have time ask, "How can we best pray for you this week?"

12. Close the meeting on time with a 1-minute prayer.

13. Make yourself available for those who wish to talk further.

About Your Last Meeting

This meeting is for review, celebration, and support. Be flexible and creative:

- Be sure to review the purpose of the **SLL**.

- Ask, "*Did God answer the prayer you wrote in the first lesson?*" Give everyone a chance to share. Celebrate answered prayers and encourage those who are still waiting.

- Help your group reflect on funny things and sad times.

Coaching

Developing an intentional coaching relationship is **NOT** part of the main responsibilities of the **SF.** But since this is a relational ministry seeking one on one encounters may lead to some coaching conversations. As part of the shepherding role, the **SF** needs to be sensitive and prepared for how and when the relationship needs to transition into a coaching relationship and be directed to the right resource. We will provide more detail in the section on Strengths Coaching. For now, we wish to stress the need for:

Listening well to understand when to ask the right questions. Since **SF** is not looking to engage in a coaching relationship, the questions need to be filled with love and compassion but

92

transitional and directive rather than open.   Your goal should be to find the next step for impacting the relationship. Here are some examples:

- *"Would you like to understand how to develop a personal relationship with Jesus?"*

- *"What do you think should be your next steps?"*

- *"Would you like to find someone skilled to help you with …?"*

- *"Do you want someone to help you go deeper in understanding your life callings?"*

- *"Would you like to invest in an intentional one on one coaching relationship?"*

Administration

The **SLL** is designed to require minimum administration. All the resources you need are provided in a simple, easy to access way. The lessons are practical and can be self-taught through the self-study web-based resources.

- **Shepherding:** Loving people. This is a most important measurement or key performance indicator given to us by Jesus when he said, *"A new commandment I give unto you, that ye love one another; as I have loved you, that ye also love one another. By this shall all men know that ye are my disciples if ye have love one to another."* John 13:34-35. Please note that this is the ONLY new commandment that Jesus gave.

- **Learning Outcome:** In what may be considered His most intimate conversation Jesus gave Peter the priority of His ministry when he asked, *"'Simon son of John, do you love me?' Peter was hurt because Jesus asked him the third time, 'Do you love me?' He said, 'Lord, you know all things; you know that I love you.' Jesus said, 'Feed my sheep.'"* John 21:17 Measuring the learning outcome will help you look for ways to grow as you enhance your facilitation skills and methods.

- **Organizational:** You are entrusted with the time given to you by each of your group members. Be careful how you manage the time and how engaged each member feels about the discussions.

About Surveys

Simple surveys can be an effective tool to provide some basic key performance indicators. It is important to make the survey confidential and anonymous. Use a few subjective, qualitative statements that reflect how your group members feel to develop a survey that requires little time and administration. Further, this input can be easily summarized using a simple Excel sheet. These results are a great discussion tool with your ministry team and overseer.

Here is one survey structure that you may adapt to your needs.

Introduction: Your input is very important to us. The Strengths Learning Lab is a journey of continuous improvement. Your candid, anonymous input will serve in helping us learn and grow. Using the (5) as strongly agree and (1) as Strongly disagree, please tell us "To what extent do you agree or disagree with the following statements?"

- The facilitator made me feel loved and appreciated.
- This group was a safe place to share, learn, and grow.
- I have learned to define and articulate my strengths.
- I have gained a process that will help me identify my life roles so I can fulfill my life callings.
- The group interaction was healthy and meaningful.
- The pace and timelines were appropriate for our objectives.
- The facilitators listened very well.
- The facilitator asked good questions.
- I would strongly recommend this group.

Also, please tell us:

- What would you say if asked about this Learning Lab?

- What would you suggest that could improve this Learning Lab?

About Ministry Term

Ministry should never be a life sentence. While the desire is for a longer-term commitment, the ministry term should be limited to a maximum of only 24 weeks.   This allows for 12-weeks of planning and training plus one 12-week semester of learning lab. Naturally, this should be confirmed by the Lord's direction and the agreement of the overseer and facilitator.

Empowerment

Empowerment is revealed in the following three dimensions:

- **Authority:** Authority is the permission for the *SF* to play his or her assigned role. God created authority and structure for the protection of His people and His kingdom. The church was established by Jesus as an expression of a biblical structure. Imperfect in its human components, it is still the most appropriate structure for the *SLL* as a ministry.

  The *SF* gains his or her authority or permission from the Ministry Overseer who in turn receives authority from another church leader such as a pastor.   This chain of command is biblical and must be respected and protected.

- **Resources:** All the teaching resources are available at the Strengths Self-Study website. The facilitator resources along with a facilitator training video are available at https://nomoreoverload.com/home/lys/sll/

- **Time:** This is the time that the *SF* must commit to this ministry. Paul admonishes us to *"Present our bodies as a living sacrifice."* Romans 12:1 This can be reflected in giving our talents and strengths to the service of God's Kingdom. Here is a simple guideline of the amount of time required during a ministry term:

- o **Weekly group meeting:** About 1.5 hours per week
  - Personal study lesson preparation
  - Time with the group
- o **Shepherding time:** Connecting with group members each week (in-person or web-based meeting)
- Weekly prayer and connection time
  - One on one relationship building time
- o **Shepherding time with overseer:** About two hours per month (in-person or web-based meeting)
- o **Time for prayer**, support, and accountability. About one hour per month.

Tell Jesus

- Go back and examine the thoughts shared in this section.

- Journal and summarize your observations. Write them down.

Write it. Share what you learned as a written conversation with Jesus. Remember, He is listening and He said I am with you always.

STRENGTHS COACHING

Playing the Role of Coach

In the three years Jesus spent in public ministry, he played many roles. While preaching and teaching, He spoke to large crowds. When He was with the 12 disciples, he enjoyed the relationship of a small group. In this setting we see him facilitating small group discussions. But I would like to suggest that His greatest impact was in His one on one encounters. Here are a few examples as we see him talking with:

- The Samaritan woman John 4:16

- The woman caught in adultery John 8:4

- Nicodemus John 3:1

- Peter and asking him, "Do you truly love me?" John 21:16

In these situations, we see the hallmarks of good coaches. In these encounters Jesus demonstrated the most important skills of good coaches; He asked good questions, He listened well, and when He spoke, He was relevant and focused.

In some ways, coaching can be confused with other professional designations such as consulting, counseling, and especially mentoring. While all of these are intentional, process-driven relationships that rely on **active listening and asking good questions,** coaching can be short term and limited in scope. It is very different from counseling or therapy which assumes a level of technical or clinical competency. Coaching can apply to any personal encounter **that seeks the best interest of the other person.**

When we consider life coaching, we observe that all coaches follow common principles, skills, and processes. But the key to successful coaching hinges on having the right focus or fit in tools, knowledge, and most related importantly personal experience.

> *Dr. Al Winseman of Gallup says that, "Every one needs a coach and every one can coach.". In a similar way, Dr. Ted Engstrom says that, "Every one needs a Paul and every one must have a Timothy.*

The following are some questions that may help you discern your coaching fit:

- What draws you to coaching?
- What topics or issues are you passionate about?
- What needs in the lives of people around you seem to interest you?
- What are you expert at or accomplished in?
- Are you a survivor of common life challenges?
- What kinds of people or needs are you most attracted to?
- What have you experienced through success and failure that you can coach others through?
- Are you living a life that you want specific individuals or groups of people to emulate?

What Do Coaches Do?

As I left home, I was a bit apprehensive about the task ahead of me. I was asked to speak to a gathering of pastors during their regional conference. The topic they had chosen was "Overcoming Overload. I was very familiar with the topic and had given the same presentation to many groups large and small. But this time, these people were different. They were pastors and their wives.

Over the years I struggled with a sense of inadequacy when talking with pastors. Since my childhood, I was taught to treat pastors with higher esteem and respect. Pastors have been my teachers and counselors. They were more educated and knowable about life than I will ever be. What did I have that they did not already know? Who was I that they would listen to me? Why would God want me to do this? He could send a more experienced pastor who could relate to challenges pastors face.

Arriving at the meeting, I prayed, "Lord, other than a presence, what role do you want me to play?"

The place was full of pastors in conversation with their friends. Nobody noticed me or said hello. This made me more self-conscious and insecure. As soon as I saw the sign, I headed for the registration desk. They gave me my name badge and pointed me to the coffee table.

As I reached for a coffee cup a woman was giving a coffee to her husband. I said the customary, *"How are you?"* He answered a quick, *"Fine, thank you."* The look on his wife's face told a different story. She asked me, *"What church do you pastor?"* Revealing my insecurity, I said, *"No I am not a pastor, I am just a ..."* Glancing at my name badged she interrupted me, *"You are one of the speakers. Your topic is very interesting, I looked at your website it is very interesting."* I was flattered and encouraged by her words. I glanced at her husband; he was silent and disengaged. I glanced at his name badge and it said, Pastor Joe ...

The organizers had me speak from 11:00-12:00 p.m. During my talk, I noticed that Pastor Joe and his wife were sitting in the second row from the front. Over the years, I learned that I could never compete with food or the call of empty stomachs. Therefore, I kept my talk short with a few exercises and a time for questions. As soon as I stepped off the stage Pastor Joe's wife came up to me and said, *"My name is Sara. My husband, Joe, and I wonder if we could have lunch together."* I agreed. She told me she would find us a table.

After meeting and talking with a few people, I went to the church gym where lunch was set up. Looking for them, I noticed them standing beside a small table in the furthest corner and they had put only three chairs at that table. Sara motioned to me to come to her table. I said to myself, *"This woman is a strategist who likes to be in control."* I cried, *"Lord, help!"* Sara offered to get our lunch boxes while we sat and talked. Since she did not give me a choice I agreed.

Sitting down, I asked him again, "How are you?" He glanced at me as if to say, *"You already asked me this at the coffee table this morning"* but then he said, *"I am fine."* I tried to make some small talk by asking about his church and family. His answer led me to believe that this was going to be a hard nut to crack so I carried on with more small talk about the weather and the good drive I had coming from my home.

Finally, Sara arrived with lunch. As I ate my lunch she opened up and complimented me on my talk and how they could relate to what I said about the risks of overloaded life. Joe was very quiet.

At a point when she paused, I looked at Joe and said, *"This morning when I asked you how you are you said, "I am fine." But what does this mean?"* This was the challenge my wife and I faced in the very busy early years of our married life. Since we were committed to honest communication we used to ask, **"How are you really, on a scale of 1-5?"**

Reaching for my wallet I pulled out my How are You Card saying, *"Over the years, this developed into a simple business size card as a conversation tool that I often share with friends and clients."*

"May I ask you, how are you really, on a scale of 1-5?" Now we do not have to discuss anything but I hope you can tell me the truth so I can pray for you. On a scale of one to five, how are you physically, emotionally, spiritually, and financially?

He looked for a moment and asked, *"Is 5 good or bad?"* I suggested, *"5 is excellent and one is very bad".* After what seemed to be a very long silence, he said, *"I guess if you were to ask my wife, she will tell you they are 1 or maybe 2 at best."*

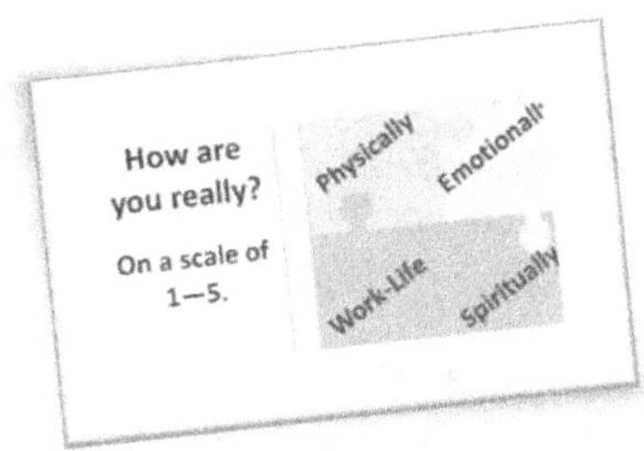

Looking at Sara, I was about to ask here for her scores, the tears in her eyes told me I should move on. So I said, *"Can I assume you must be going through a rough patch in life or ministry?"*

With this Joe opened up telling me that he had been on sick leave for the past 4 months. He told me that his doctor and a counselor had told him that the stress of ministry was causing great stress in his life. Sara interjected that several family members told him to look for a different career.

At this, Joe interrupted her, *"I cannot leave the pastorate. This is my calling."* For almost 10 minutes, I listened as they debated. Occasionally I interjected trying to identify roles and responsibilities that may be the cause of his greatest stress.

Coming near the end, I said, *"Joe, can you tell me how many times Jesus was called 'pastor?'"* As he looked, I replied, **"Not even once."** I went on to explain that "pastor" as a church title embodies many roles. Some of these roles a good fit for your God-given strengths and they energize you. Others are not a good fit for your God-given talents and they drain you.

With that, I drew the attached Venn diagram[9] saying, *"Joe, in your life and the life of every one of us we play a MIX of these three types of roles."*

- **"Relational roles** *involve mostly one on one interactions where you play the role of a counselor, coach, and mentor.*

- **Project roles** *involve working with others to bring about change. You may play the role of manager, coordinator, and organizer. In the church, you will see this in mission trips, evangelization programs, and building projects.*

- **In the operational space**, *you are likely to be involved in repetitive, predictable, or routine-oriented tasks. In church life, they appear in preaching, finance, and administration."*

Glancing at Sara, she was already taking notes. Turning to Joe I said, *"Based on your natural talents, which of these areas energize you and which ones drain you?"* The conversation that followed between Joe and his wife revealed that Pastor Joe knew himself very well. I learned that he had a Master's degree in divinity with a minor in counseling. He knew what energized him and what drained him but was trapped in a title-driven world that imposed roles and tasks that conflicted with his God-given Strengths.

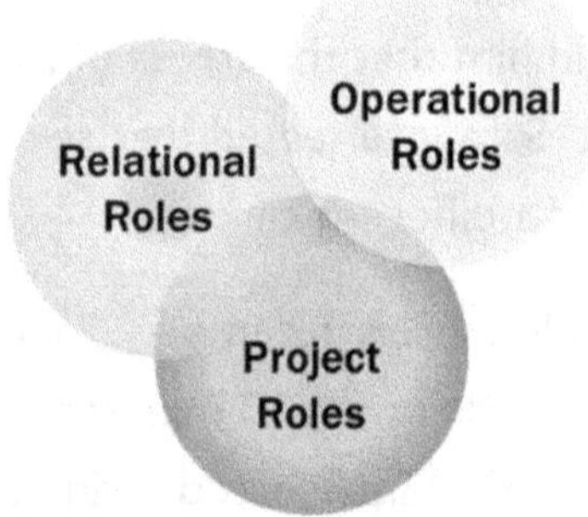

Looking at him I said, "Joe, how can you create balance in your work-life with a balance between roles that energize you and roles that drain you?" He said, *"This is exactly my problem; I am trapped and I cannot get out."*

---

[9] See Appendix for links to several time budgeting and management tools.

Looking at him I said, "Joe, may I remind you that *"No temptation has overtaken you that is not common to man. God is faithful, and He will not let you be tempted beyond your ability, but with the temptation, He will also provide the way of escape, that you may be able to endure it."* I Corinthians 10:13

Going further I shared with Joe and Sara, how the title of Pastor and Pastor's Wife embodies many roles. Because you are human, you are called to a specific role for which you are best equipped by the unique talents God has given you. The rest are human expectations, or what we like to call **"Title Imposed Roles"**. These are not your callings. Our identity does not come from our title but from playing the best roles Jesus calls us to play.

Feeling some empathy for Joe, I asked, *"Pastor Joe, how can I help you?"* He answered, *"I do not know; I guess this is my cross and I have to carry it."* Looking at Sara, her eyes spoke of hopelessness and fear for her husband.

Trying to bring some hope I said, *"Joe, you do not need to feel trapped in such a stressful career. I suspect you already know what you should do. You can change. Your doctor and family members have given you good advice. You know that change will have a price. The question I have for you is are you willing to pay the price of change?"* Looking at his wife he said, *"I told you, I always wanted to be a pastor. This is who I am. This is who God called me to be. I am not going to change that."*

At that moment I knew my role with Joe had come to an end. Handing him my business card I said, "At *our website, we have a self-study course that may help you focus your roles on your God-given Strengths. Feel free to access anything you may find there."*

After our meeting, Joe downloaded our free books from our website, so I phoned him to see if he had any questions. He did not return my call.   Three years later, I learned that 6 months after returning from his sick leave Joe was fired from his church and moved to another town where he now works as a fulltime counselor.

Coaches Listen Well

In the very famous prayer of Saint Francis he says, *"O Divine Master, grant that I may not so much seek to be consoled as to console; **to be understood as to understand**; to be loved as to love. For it is in giving that we receive…"*

In his book, *Effective Coaching: Lessons from the Coaches' Coach,* Myles Downey writes, **"The primary function of the Coach is to understand. Not to solve, fix, heal, make better, or be wise. But to understand. The magic is that it is in that moment of understanding, the Client[10] understands for himself, becomes more aware, and is then in a position to make better decisions and choices than he would have done anyway. This is how Coaching is profoundly simple and simply profound."[11]**

Understanding comes from good listening. You may have heard it said that communication is 10% words (verbal), 30% tone (vocal), and 60% body language (visual). These are often called the 3V's of good communication. Good listening also involves not only the ears but the heart and the eyes as well. To become an effective listener, you must first care wholeheartedly.

> **'People don't care how much you know until they know how much you care."**
> **Theodore Roosevelt**

---

[10] In this section we will use the term "client" as a reference to others.

[11] Myles Downey, *Effective Coaching: Lessons from the Coaches 'Coach* (South Melbourne, Australia: Cengage Learning, 2003), 59.

In our busy life, sometimes this is not easy. To help you develop good listening here are some tips that you can practice with family friends and of course, coaching clients.

- Make strong eye contact.

- Listen to understand, not only to learn.

- Tell the client, "Let me see if I understood you correctly" or

- Tell your client "Let me tell you what I think I heard you say."

- Listen to the tone of voice and the emotions that hide behind the words.

- Listen prayerfully. Remember, Jesus is part of the conversation. Ask the Lord to reveal to you what He knows.

- Let your body language communicate that you are listening.

- Remove all distractions so both you and your client can focus on each other.

- Most importantly listen with love. Love shows through your own words and body language.

"Love never gives up. Love cares more for others than for self. Love doesn't want what it doesn't have. Love doesn't strut, Doesn't have a swelled head, Doesn't force itself on others, Isn't always "my first," Doesn't fly off the handle, Doesn't keep score of the sins of others, Doesn't revel when others grovel, Takes pleasure in the flowering of truth, puts up with anything, Trusts God always. Always looks for the best, Never looks back, But keeps going to the end." I Corinthians 13:4-7 MSG. Love is hard; you cannot do it so **"ask God to love your client through you."**

Question:

- If you asked the people closest to you to rate your listening skills what would they say? Why not ask them? Here is a simple way.

- Using Google Forms, you can create a FREE, anonymous survey that you can send to your family and friends. In their response, they do not have to provide any identity. The following is a sample DRAFT survey content.

Coaches Ask Good Questions

Good questions speak more than words. They communicate interest, curiosity, and how you value the person you are talking with, and most importantly, they express your sincerity.

> **Questions are more powerful than answers.**

"Questions have the power to change lives. They can jump-start creativity, change our perspective, and empower us to believe in ourselves - push us to think things through or call us to action."[12] Asking the right questions and ensuring the client provides candid answers are the life-blood of a coaching session. This reveals the true skill of a Coach and the Client's readiness to change.

Questions encourage the Client to think. They help him or her move to a clearer state of awareness and uncover hidden solutions. Also, questions help the Client understand the realities and the responsibilities associated with the issues or goals he or she faces. Questions are a powerful tool to create focus, articulate assumptions, and qualify risks - as well as transitioning to actions that achieve desired outcomes.

> **Without being manipulative, if you have an opinion, rephrase it into a revealing question to help your clients think and discover answers.**

The Coach must often rely heavily on open-ended questions that start with **how, what, why, who, or when**.

---

[12] Tony Stoltzfus, *Coaching Questions: A Coach's Guide to Powerful Asking Skills* (Virginia Beach, VA: Tony Stoltzfus, 2008), 7.

Similar to what we provided in the section on facilitation, the following are examples of the many types of questions a Coach might employ:

- **Revealing questions** encourage creativity and imagination. They invite the Client to think differently. Revealing questions seek to challenge limitations, beliefs, and established priorities.

    o   Where are you right now concerning…?

    o   What do you like about where you are now…?

    o   What don't you like about where you are now…?

    o   What do you care about most deeply regarding…?

    o   What are your unique strengths, skills, experiences…?

    o   How did you feel about…?

    o   What other pictures can you see when you think of…?

    o   What values do you hold most dear…?

    o   Who else can you consider for…?

- **Ownership questions** encourage the client to take responsibility, be more proactive, or define **"SMART"** goals and action steps.

    o   What part are you playing in…?

    o   What have you done that contributed to…?

    o   What is it that you could have done differently…?

    o   What do you want to do about…?

    o   How can you change…?

- **Direct questions** seek focus, action, and/or accountability. When used wisely, these questions can help ensure that the coaching session provides the greatest benefit to the Client.

    o   What progress will you make regarding…?

- o How will you communicate...?

- o What are you prepared to do next...?

- o When do you plan to...?

- o How can we be sure that you will...?

- o How can you share the change you are making to help others facing similar challenges?

Learn more at:

https://www.youtube.com/watch?v=sGv-moiGZps

https://www.youtube.com/watch?v=J8xfuCcXZu8

https://www.youtube.com/watch?v=5K842cXNIEl

https://www.youtube.com/watch?v=u6GtXjpeGl4

Question: If you asked the people closest to you to rate your skill in asking questions, what would they say? **Why not ask them?**

Coaches Follow A Good Process

Unlike my meeting with Pastor Joe, which was driven by his wife, my meeting with Daniel started on a long bus ride home after a busy day.

He said, *"Long day, eh?"*
I replied, *"Long but good."*
With a friendly grin, he asked, *"What kind of work do you do?"*
I replied, *"I help people struggling with work and information overload."*
With a curious look, he said, *"Wow, tell me more. How do you do that?"*

"When people understand their Strengths and define and focus on roles that are a good match to their natural talents, this energizes them and does not overload them and the opposite is true"

By the end of our 50-minute bus ride, I learned about his role and that he leads a staff of about 300 people who all seem to struggle with excessive work demands. Before leaving we exchanged business cards and agreed to meet at his office the following week.

The following is a paraphrase of some of the conversations I had with Daniel during our first meeting.

Me: *"Daniel, may I ask you, what is your role at ABX Co?"*

Daniel: *"I am the Director of Operations."*

Me: *"This is your title, but what is your role?"*

Daniel: *"I am responsible for all aspects of the supply change."*

Me: *"Sorry, this is your responsibility, but how do you describe the key roles you play during a given day?"*

Daniel: *"I am not sure, because my role depends on what each day brings and what people I have to deal with."*

Me: *"I appreciate your honesty. What I think I heard you say is that you play many roles. Can you tell me which one best describes your average day? For example, I will give you five roles and you tell me the one that best describes your average day. Is that Ok?"*

Daniel: *"Sure."*

Me: *"In your relationships with your 10 managers are you a boss, manager, leader, firefighter, troubleshooter, coach, overseer, or policeman?"*

Daniel: *"Are you asking me what I am or what I wish to be?"*

Me: *"Perfect answer. Thank you. Give me both; what you are now and what do you wish to be?"*

As we discussed the meaning of each of these roles, Daniel could see that his main challenge was that he allowed others to see him as a firefighter, policeman, and troubleshooter. He was able to see that it was defining his role, not his title, and it defined not only how others saw him but also what they expected of him. He began to understand that his role defined what he did but more importantly, how he did it and the information he collected in the process. Through that simple interaction, Daniel quickly realized the cause of his work and information overload.

Through further discussion, he assured me that he could see his greatest contribution would be in playing the role of an **overseer** and **coach**.   That meeting in April 2004 with Daniel started a long-term relationship. As I coached Daniel in redefining his roles and work life, he applied the same coaching with his managers who applied it with their staff. The results exceeded all of our expectations.

> *In effective coaching the client controls the objectives and goals; the coach controls the process and tools.*

The Process

As a purpose-driven relationship, the coaching process is very similar to the facilitation process. Once you go beyond the informal casual introductions that may happen on a bus, church, or first office meeting, you, as the Coach, must set clear expectations of a disciplined, process-oriented relationship.

In the following section we will share with you a transferable process which we have applied with large clients such as IBM and Xerox as well as pastors and their small pastoral teams. The process is adapted from a model that is used by most life and executive coaches around the world.

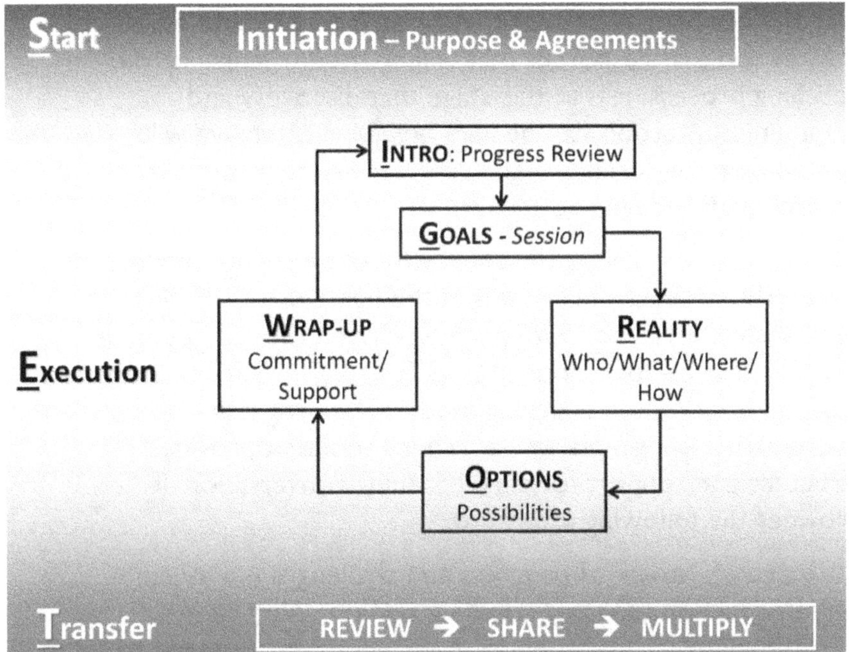

Because of our God-given talents and strengths, we tend to be more structured in our coaching style than other coaches may be. This appeals to some clients but may not appeal to others.

The above diagram illustrates a process that we will describe in the following pages. We hope that you will adopt this framework for your style and client needs.

You will note that the attached image includes two difference processes defined by the two words **"SET"** and "**I GROW**":

SET (**S**tart, **E**xecution, and **T**ransfer), illustrated in the attached diagram, highlight the elements that contribute to a successful and transferable coaching relationship.

1. **S**TART: The beginning of a relationship sets the stage for its success or failure. After a casual introduction or meetings, the initiation meeting is the first step towards ensuring a fit between Coach and Client. It the time when a common purpose is defined, needs are uncovered, and objectives are communicated. As soon as possible, the Coach and Client must agree on confidentiality, meeting frequency, and how

long the coaching relationship will last. It is helpful to agree on the key tools or resources that will be used to enhance the coaching process. It is at this stage that discovery and communication tools can be very helpful.[13] Later, we will discuss how the Strengths coaching can relate to the two critical needs we defined earlier.

2. **EXECUTION:** This is the stage where the rubber hits the road. This repeated process is at the heart of a Coaching relationship. It is a series of purpose-driven conversations or sessions that use the model: "**I G R O W**". GROW is the most widely adapted coaching model. The Progress Dashboard[14] is a simple low-overhead tool that provides structure and support for each coaching conversation. It provides the following:

   a. **Intro:** A review of progress and challenges is a valuable introduction to every coaching session. With caring, accountability, and support, the Client is encouraged to persevere in reaching agreed-upon objectives.

   b. **Goal**: It is the responsibility of the Client to articulate clear goals for the coaching session. Focusing on goals that are **SMART** (**S**pecific, **M**easurable, **A**ttainable, **R**elevant, and **T**ime-dependent) is critical to successful Coaching conversations.

   c. **Reality:** Here, the Coach guides the Client in painting a true picture of the reality he faces. Use open-ended, revealing questions such as: "What's the real problem with...?", "Who else is involved in...?", "What happens if...?", "How do you feel about...?", and "Where would you...?" This technique ignites the Client's creativity. Understanding arises out of his or her internal resources, which may not have otherwise occurred.

   d. **Options**: As the Client uncovers the reality of issues, people, feelings, opportunities, and obstacles, many solutions and opportunities will emerge. With skillful understanding, the most appropriate options will become

---

[13] See the Appendix for the initiation exercises and template.

[14] See the Appendix for a link to download this Progress Dashboard.

clear. Now the Client is ready to make commitments and take action. Here the coach will use **ownership questions** to help the client see what he or she can do, such as, "What can you consider ...?" "What is likely to happen if ...?" "Who should you see to...?" What would happen if you ...?" "What steps can you take to ...?"

e. **Wrap up**: As the Client defines action-plans and commits to timely execution, the Coach will play an encouraging and supportive role. Even in client-directed Coaching, where a Coach does not assume much authority, the Coach must exercise (and the Client must accept) **supportive accountability**. This is essential. To help the client move to committed action plans the coach will use **direct questions** such as, "What are you prepared to do ...?" "Which of these options will you take ...?" "When will you...?" "How will you do ...?"

Note: A good coaching conversation is never about the Coach. It is always about the Client. A good Coach seeks to speak less than 20% allowing the client to speak more than 80% of the time they spend together.

3. **T**RANSFER: It has been said, *"If you want to be a master of an art, teach it."* Here we like to say, *"If you want to be a master of what you learned, coach it."* The greatest impact will happen when the Client begins to coach others in the application of what they have learned. This starts a new coaching relationship between Coach and Client. This is where the command of Jesus to *"go and make disciples"* (Matthew 28) merges with the command of Paul in 2 Timothy 2:2 *"And the things you have heard me say in the presence of many witnesses entrust to reliable men who will also be qualified to teach others."*

Coaches Use Good Tools

In the Development Framework we discussed earlier we highlighted the importance of having a good fit. Wise coaches seek to have tools that leverage their Strengths and respond to specific client needs. As a result, you will find that the list of coaching specialties is vast and may include career coaching, financial coaching, mental health coaching, health and wellness coaching, spiritual coaching, and more. Within each of these categories, a coach may even have a more defined practice. The more specialized the coach can be, the fewer tools he or she will need.

For example, while we started our practice with a broader definition of "Overcoming Overload" now our practice is focused specifically on knowing your Strengths and living your Strengths. While we both have an interest in this space, we are different because of our experiences.

In the world of the Strengths, movement coaches have specialized in a variety of fields and specialties including marriage, children, students, addiction, government, healthcare, and even long-term incarceration.

For example, where I am most effective is in the area of work-life balance and the application of strengths to defining organizational roles. For an example, we will review few of the tools we use for this specific coaching specialty later in this section.

For now, I wish to highlight generic tools. These you may like to adapt and may be helpful regardless of your coaching specialty.

Discovery Tools

Discovery tools are often used as part of the initiation process or the first phase of the coaching relationship. They are designed to help the client understand himself and communicate his or her needs. As an example, you will find in the appendix a link to a template that we have used which we call "**Initiation Exercises**." Through this reflection tool the client is encouraged to think and write answers to key questions which include the following:

1. **How are you?** The client is encouraged to write his or her honest observation of the results from the Wellness Gauge.

2. **Tell me about yourself:**

   a. What are your core values? Through this exercise, the client is expected to define the five keywords that define his or her core value and if possible, shape them into a mission statement.

   b. How would you describe your faith journey?

   c. What are your top Strengths?[15]

   d. What are your Spiritual Gifts based on the Spiritual Gifts Test? [16]

   e. What are your love languages based on the 5 Love Languages Test?[17]

3. **What are your coaching objectives and why?**

4. **How much time are you prepared to invest** per week in this coaching relationship?

The Progress Dashboard

In the Appendix, you will find a link to download the dashboard template. The purpose of this template is to provide a process that directs each coaching conversation. We like to call this **"client directed coaching."** We assume that the client directs the coaching objectives and the goal for each coaching session and the Coach directs the process and related tools. This tool provides each coaching session with a structure and a communication template. **Prepared by the Client,** this template offers an opportunity to reflect and document progress and challenges. It is also a way to communicate to the Coach where to best invest the limited time of each coaching session.

---

[15] See Appendix for link to Strengths Discovery Tool.

[16] See Appendix for link to The Spiritual Gifts Test.

[17] See Appendix for link to 5 Love Languages Test.

This template provides a simple five-part coaching process illustrated in the earlier sections:

1. **The Introduction** helps the Client respond to the important **"How are you?"** question. How the Client feels sets the tone and priorities of a caring relationship. To lend a bit of objectivity, the Client is encouraged to indicate, on a scale of 1 – 5, how he or she feels physically, emotionally, spiritually, and relating to work life.

To help provide continuity from one session to the next, the Client is encouraged to record and share:

- Lessons learned about his or her Strengths and their application.

- Accomplishments since the last session, as well as any challenges or obstacles that have been encountered.

Depending on what is shared and the time available, the Coach may use these as a springboard for further discussion.

Goal setting is important. Coaching time is limited. Goal setting ensures that the Client defines what he would like to achieve by the end of the coaching session.

2. **Coaching discussion notes** help the Client and the Coach remember important and helpful thoughts for follow-up, support, and accountability.

- **Reality discussion** is a place to record an understanding of the issues at hand.

- **Options discussion** is a place to record and narrow down the choices available, and the impact of each, before agreeing on the best action plan.

- **Wrapping up the coaching session** records specific actions the Client is prepared to take. The Coach may ask the Client questions like these:

- o So, what would you like to do?

- o Is this what you commit to doing?

- o When do you expect to do it…?

- o How will I know you have done it?

Coaching for Self-Esteem

There are strong indicators that the majority of people you and I meet every day struggle with self-esteem. According to a survey by the International Federation of Coaches, Self-esteem is the number one reason for which people seek the help of life or executive coaches. If you ask Google you will learn that 85% of people struggle with self-esteem.

The Strengths Workshop tool includes coaching questions and thinking exercises to help individuals overcome this temptation and build their self-esteem. Using these as tools along with the coaching process we outlined earlier will help you impact teachable people or clients God may bring your way.

Identity in Relationships

Leading media, as well as social media, would influence us to believe that our identity is based on what we do or what we own. This is furthest from the truth. Leading psychologists tell us that the greatest help to the problem of self-esteem comes from being valued in healthy relationships and communities.

Affirmed by God

Being affirmed by an almighty God could be the most powerful antidote to the problem of low self-esteem. The Strengths Workshop is biblically founded on Genesis 1:26 and the fact that we are uniquely created in God's image.

Also, it is often helpful for the client to study and meditate on who they are in God and Christ using verses like:

- I am God's beloved child (John 1:12).
- I am Christ's dear friend (John 15:5).
- I am filled with the fullness of Christ (Ephesians 3:19).
- I am holy and blameless (Ephesians 1:3).
- I am made perfect forever (Hebrews 10:14).
- I am the salt of the Earth (Matthew 5:13).
- I am the light of the world (Matthew 5:14).
- I am a citizen of heaven (Philippians 3:20).
- I am inseparable from God's love (Romans 8:35-39).
- I am filled with the peace and joy of God (Romans 14:7).
- I am a co-worker with God (1 Corinthians 3:9).
- I am a priest of the highest God (1 Pet 3:5-9).

Affirmed by Important People

Taking inventory of healthy relationships is a powerful tool in building our self-esteem. In the Strengths Development toolset, we provide some exercises to help the client leverage a relationship with the important and teachable people.

Further, defining clear and well-communicated roles plays a vital part in building one's self-esteem. The role development template is based on understanding how we collaborate with others and the value we bring in interdependent relationships.

Going Deeper in Strengths

Strengths Discovery is a lifelong journey. The field of Strengths Psychology offers a growing set of tools and resources that can help clients be affirmed in their uniqueness and value. We will provide links to these resources along with thinking and coaching exercises to support the coaches' role.

Coaching for Work-Life Balance

In the survey by the International Coaching Federation, 36% of coaches surveyed indicate that work-life balance is the primary reason for which clients seek the services of a life coach. Also, 73% of coaches surveyed report that dealing with work-life balance issues is important in how they seek to help their clients.

While work-life balance may be a myth, the goal is to create an integrated, balanced life following the model of Jesus. The coaching tools we will offer you will help you guide your clients in identifying roles, relationships, and tasks that energize and support them as they face the ones that are likely to drain them.

Finding Your Sweet Spot at Work

Our work-life is changing every day. In North America, the average work tenure is less than 4.2 years. The gig economy is the fastest-growing segment of all sectors. Leveraging the healthy process of change management along with the development framework, we will provide you

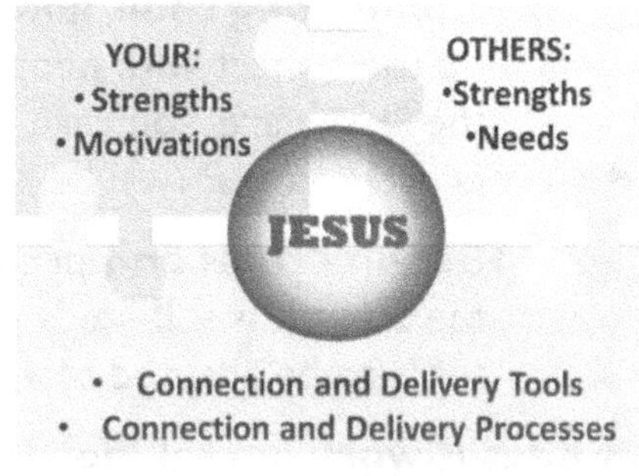

with some coaching questions to help you guide your clients in this changing world.

Application: What Can You Do?

The stories we shared with you so far highlight that you do not need to have a title to be a Coach. Do you know anyone who:

- Is struggling with self-worth or self-esteem issues?

- Is discouraged with work-life balance?

- Do you know someone who is going through a possible job change?

Examining the ministry development framework, do you know anyone who needs coaching? Give that person a name. Let us call him Jack. With Jesus as your guide, consider the following:

- **About you: What Strengths and Motivation?**
    - What natural talents? Use adjectives to describe them.
    - What Knowledge + Skill + Experience will help you relate to Jack?
    - What are your motivations? Why would you wish to help Jack?

- **About your Jane:** What Strengths (Talents X Knowledge + Skills + Experience) has she been given? What are her needs or life challenges?

- **About tools and processes:** I would like you to think of:
    - **Connecting tools and processes.** What can you do to connect with people like Jane? How can you use the "How are You card" or the Wellness Gauge as effective tools?
    - **Serving tools and processes:** How can you best use the Strengths self-study tools? Remember these are tools to be adapted to your style and need.

How does it work in real life? The tools and processes we have shared so far have proven to be highly transferable. You can adapt them to help students, as well those in full-time work. They are also culturally adaptable to different levels of mental and intellectual capacity. Having said that, effective coaching hinges on the ability to focus on the coach's sweet spot.

About Jesus: Remember, there is never a perfect fit. Jesus will fill in the gaps. He is more than able. How would you like to ask Him to help you so you can help your Jane?

Application: What is Your Role?

Usually, we feel very inadequate when separated by many miles. We may often fear the risk of misunderstanding or miscommunicating. This inadequacy can be reduced when you know that Jesus is your partner in this process. With His help, He can guide you as you

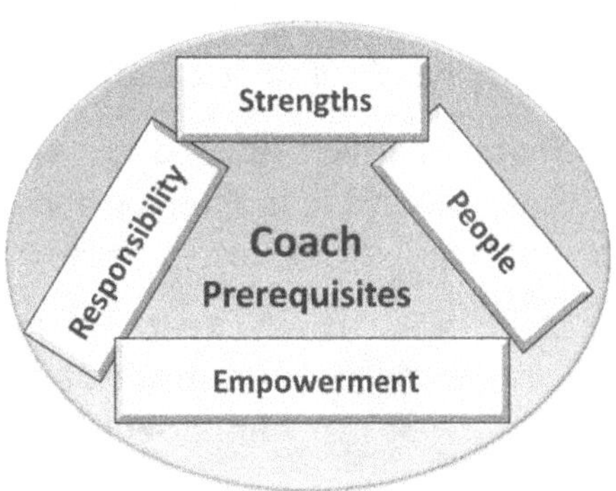

FOCUS on coaching relationships where you can be most effective. Here are some questions to guide you in defining your role.

- **Coach Prerequisites:** What are the specific prerequisite qualifications for your coaching role?

- **Strengths:** What Strengths do you bring to your focused coaching relationships?
    - o   What natural talents? Use adjectives to describe them.
    - o   What knowledge + skills + experience will most likely relate to Jane?

- **Who are the people** in your role?
    - o   Who are the partners who will support you?
    - o   Who are the teachable people, or clients, other than Jack that you may consider helping? What are their Strengths and needs?

- **What responsibilities** do you have? What are you accountable for?

- **What empowerment** do you need? Be sure to consider tools and resources as well as how much time you are prepared to invest or spend with Jack.

Tell Jesus

- Go back and examine the thoughts shared in this section.

- Journal and summarize your observations. Write them down.

- Share what you learned as a written conversation with Jesus. Remember, He is listening and He said I am with you always.

Write it. Tell Jesus what you would like to do as a result of what you have learned. Tell Him how you want Him to help you.

APPENDIX

Tools and Templates

- **How are You Card -** https://nomoreoverload.com/Data-Web/Notes/HowAreYou.pdf
- **Wellness Gauge –** https://nomoreoverload.com/home/lys/sdc/wg/
- **Coaching Initiation Exercise**
- **Progress Dashboard** https://nomoreoverload.com/Data-Web/Templates/PrgDash.Personal.doc
- **Time Management Tool**
    - **Week at a glance (Paper Calendar)** https://nomoreoverload.com/Data-Web/Templates/WeeK%20at%20a%20glance.XLS
    - **Weekly Time Planning** https://nomoreoverload.com/Data-Web/Templates/Weekly-Planner.xls
    - **Yearly Time Planning** https://nomoreoverload.com/Data-Web/Templates/Yearly-Planner.xls

Papers References and Links

- See our free bookstore http://es.nomoreoverload.com/